RAILWAY
DEPOTS, STATIONS & TERMINALS

BRIAN SOLOMON

Voyageur Press

To the memory of Charles Richard Neumiller

First published in 2015 by Voyageur Press, an imprint of Quarto Publishing Group USA Inc., 400 First Avenue North, Suite 400, Minneapolis, MN 55401 USA

The information in this book is true and complete to the best of our knowledge. All recommendations are made without any guarantee on the part of the author or Publisher, who also disclaims any liability incurred in connection with the use of this data or specific details.

We recognize, further, that some words, model names, and designations mentioned herein are the property of the trademark holder. We use them for identification purposes only. This is not an official publication.

Voyageur Press titles are also available at discounts in bulk quantity for industrial or sales-promotional use. For details write to Special Sales Manager at Quarto Publishing Group USA Inc., 400 First Avenue North, Suite 400, Minneapolis, MN 55401 USA.

To find out more about our books, visit us online at www.voyageurpress.com.

ISBN: 978-0-7603-4890-1

Library of Congress Cataloging-in-Publication Data

Solomon, Brian, 1966-
  Railway depots, stations, & terminals / by Brian Solomon.
    pages cm
  Includes bibliographical references and index.
  ISBN 978-0-7603-4890-1 (hc)
  1. Railroad stations--History. I. Title.
  TF300.S6753 2015
  385.3'1409--dc23
                                        2015011951

Acquiring Editor: Todd R. Berger
Project Manager: Caitlin Fultz and Alyssa Bluhm
Art Director: Cindy Samargia Laun
Cover Designer: Karl Laun
Book Designer: John Barnett/4 Eyes Design
Layout: Rebecca Pagel

Front cover: © Blaine Harrington III / Alamy

Back cover: Brian Solomon (corner images), Tom Kline (center)

Front jacket flap: Brian Solomon (left), Patrick Yough (right)

Back jacket flap: Brian Solomon (both)

On the frontis: Fellheimer and Wagner's masterpiece at Cincinnati was considered for demolition, thankfully the station was preserved and restored and in 1990 was re-opened as the Cincinnati Museum Center. *Brian Solomon*

On the title page: This view of Hoboken's main waiting room was exposed during the midday lull on January 15, 2015. Architect Kenneth W. Murchison was a student of the École des Beaux-Arts in Paris and was inspired by the French Baroque for his styling of the station. Hoboken Terminal underwent an extensive restoration between 2004 and 2011 that included work on its ferry slips. *Brian Solomon*

Printed in China

10 9 8 7 6 5 4 3 2 1

CONTENTS

ACKNOWLEDGMENTS

Over the course of more than four decades of railroad photography, I've sought out and visited hundreds of examples of railway architecture across North America, Europe, and Japan. During this time, a great many people have fostered my interest in railways and railway stations. This book is a culmination of these efforts.

Special thanks to my father, Richard Jay Solomon, for bringing me on my earliest railway trips and many in recent years, for the use of his extensive library and photographs, and for proofreading drafts of this text. My brother Seán has often accompanied me on railway trips, and we've spent more than two decades exploring stations in North America, Spain, and elsewhere. My mother, Maureen Solomon, has often met me at stations and was especially patient of my railway adventures in my younger days. On one occasion she collected me in the gloom, after midnight on an October evening at the Palmer Union Station on my arrival in the locomotive cab on freight from New London, Connecticut.

Many people have helped me over the years in my quest for information and details concerning railroad operations and infrastructure. Pat Yough lent me the use of his library, provided photographs, and traveled with me to investigate many stations. John Gruber and I have explored stations in Pennsylvania, Ohio, Illinois, Iowa, Nebraska, Wisconsin, and California, as well as in Poland and Germany, and John has also supplied text and photography for this book. Jack May provided tours of New Jersey stations.

Thanks to the late Robert A. Buck of Tucker's Hobbies for encouraging my railroad interest in regard to his favorite Boston & Albany line and elsewhere across America. Markku Pulkkinen helped with details and proofreading on Helsinki's main station. Tessa Bold traveled with me in England, Germany, and Sweden and met me at railway stations in all three countries. The members of the Irish Railway Record Society provided me with unrestricted access to their Dublin library and answered numerous questions about buildings in Ireland, Britain, and elsewhere around the world. Special thanks to Denis McCabe, Ken Fox, Colm O'Callaghan, David Hegarty, Dan Smith, Gerry Conmy,

Stephen Hirsch, and Oliver Doyle. Visits to the United Kingdom have been aided by Hassard Stacpoole, Milepost 92.5's Colin and James Garratt, and the late Colin Nash. Thanks to Colin Horan for visits to Belgium and the Netherlands. My appreciation to John P. Hankey and Paul Hammond for providing me a detailed visit to the Baltimore area and lending considerable knowledge about the history of railroads in that cradle of American railroading. Thanks to Amtrak's Joe Burgess for tours of New England stations and to George C. Corey, Tim Doherty, and Tom Kline for their photography. Dennis LeBeau let me borrow photographs from the William Bullard Archive and provided tours of central Massachusetts. Doug Riddell hosted me on visits to Virginia, provided me tours of Washington Union Station, gave me valuable connections in North Carolina, and supplied material and photos included in the book. Photographers and collection are credited in the captions. My cousin Stella Castillo hosted me in southern California and joined me in exploration of stations in southern Vermont. Tom Hargadon hosted me on visits to California. The Railroad Museum of Pennsylvania's Kurt Bell and Nick Zmijewski aided my researching efforts. Clark Johnson Jr. has provided many connections and railroad trips via his private car *Caritas*.

Over the years, I've often traveled across North America with fellow photographers, including the late Mike Abalos, Howard Ande, Marshall Beecher, Phil Brahms, Mike and Tom Danneman, Doug Eisele, Paul Goewey, Chris Guss, Mike Gardner, Neal Gage, Don Gulbrandsen, Tom Hoover, Brian Jennison, Bill Keay, Bill Linley, Bob Karambelas, Blair Kooistra, George W. Kowanski, Don Marson, Doug Moore, Dan Munson, Mel Patrick, John Peters, George and Candy Pitarys, Pete Reusch, Rich Reed, J. D. Schmid, Dean Sauvola, Chris Southwell, Carl Swanson, Justin Tognetti, Otto Vondrak, and Norman Yellin.

Special thanks to Todd R. Berger, Caitlin Fultz, Cindy Laun, and everyone else at Voyageur Press for helping to transform ideas, text, and illustrations into the book that you hold in your hands.

INTRODUCTION

A railway station, be it a small country depot or monumental urban terminal, is a special kind of place. The station is a nexus; it is where travel begins and ends or makes a transition. It is a crossroads of commerce; it is where the engineer meets the architect. It is the face of the railroad in the eyes of the public. Properly speaking, a station is a location rather than a structure, a point that has led to considerable confusion over the years (explored in Chapter 2). For clarification, this book is focused on passenger station architecture and examines the styles and applications and re-adaptations and repurposing of buildings used at stations, as well as covering their planners, architects, and builders.

Railway station buildings are peculiar structures. Most, by virtue of their functional arrangement, must have two main entrances: One that faces the railway line, and one that faces the community served. Over the years, necessity has mandated considerable variation in station arrangements, sometimes complicated by tracks and entrances on multiple levels, with station facilities variously located at grade, above, and below track level. Passenger stations may be standalone structures or combined with other buildings.

Large terminals, such as those featured in Chapter 1, have incorporated a great variety of functions into station structures; they have served as markets, offices, hotels, nodes for mail distribution, and multimodal transportation hubs. These may contain a great variety of facilities, from baths to restaurants, and have often spurred urban development around them. Likewise, small stations have often played important roles in railroad operations, while serving as both freight and passenger facilities.

The railway concept was developed in Britain where, during the 1820s, the first public railways were established. These employed the recently perfected reciprocating steam locomotive engine to power trains operated on predetermined schedules. From the beginning, the station was an important part of the railway.

The railway station was adapted from earlier transportation nodes, incorporating qualities of the roadside inn, toll gates, harbors, and canal locks. Passenger services took their operational cues from

The balloon-style train shed in Köln (Cologne), Germany, is one of the longest of its type and dates from the 1890s when train shed stations were built in Germany. It is unusual today because the station facilities are located on a lower level and below the shed and tracks rather than in an adjacent building. *Brian Solomon*

practices established by both stagecoach and maritime shipping, yet rapidly developed their own peculiarities.

Limitations imposed by railway infrastructure demanded regimented operation. Trains could only pass or overtake one another where tracks were in place to facilitate these moves. As a result, operations were conducted by a strictly enforced code of rules in which the station and its staff played a crucial role.

The railway concept was exported to nations around the world. While variations in operating practices soon emerged, the essential principles remained constant. The United States was the first nation outside of Britain to embrace the railway on a large scale, and here railways were largely known as "railroads."

In the nineteenth century, the term *road* was often used to describe the railroad and not the highway. While the terms *railroad* and *railway* have often been used interchangeably in corporate names, historically in North America the heavy lines, those traditionally powered by steam locomotives, are generally known as rail*road*s. "Rail*way*" has been used to describe lightly built lines including streetcar companies, rapid transit, and industrial tramways. By contrast in Britain and continental Europe, *railway* is often used to describe the heavy lines. In this book, *railroad station* is used for most North American facilities, and *railway station* is used for facilities in Europe and the rest of the world, where the term *railroad* is not generally used.

STATION EVOLUTION

In the past two centuries, railways have undergone a multitude of changes. In the industrialized nations, railways developed rapidly and by the mid-nineteenth century they had assumed a dominant role in transportation. The mode remained the predominant means of land transport until the emergence of paved roads and gasoline-powered automobiles gradually assumed supremacy. As railways lost out to automobiles and highways, and later to airplanes for long-distance travel, the role of individual stations changed.

Baltimore & Ohio was America's first common carrier railroad line. In 1827 it was chartered from Baltimore to the Ohio River. By 1830 its line reached Ellicott's Mills (now Ellicott City) 13 miles west of Baltimore. This typical early American town was for a short while B&O's western terminus, and today it is the location of America's oldest remaining railway station. It is shown during its November 1996 rededication ceremony. *Brian Solomon*

The twin-span metal and glass train shed at Prague's Hlavní Nádraží (Main Station) as seen in May 2000. For decades, architectural enthusiasts largely ignored railway stations in Central Europe. *Brian Solomon*

In North America, as ridership declined, railroad companies scaled back passenger services and closed lightly used stations and routes. These changes are detailed in Chapters 3 and 4. By contrast, European railways and stations evolved along different paths, as discussed in Chapter 5.

While there are many common trends in railway evolution, every station has a unique history with its own timeline. Some stations prospered early and have survived into the twenty-first century and continue to grow. Others were built late, were closed early, and never met the expectations of their planners. Stations have been variously expanded and scaled back, relocated or closed, abandoned or repurposed, demolished or rebuilt. As with any important infrastructure, changes to railway stations have often incurred intense discussion, argument, and controversy.

THE ROLE OF THE STATION

Today's generation, accustomed to Internet access on portable devices where detailed and up-to-date information can be obtained anywhere and at any time, may find it difficult to appreciate the traditional importance of the station and a station agent.

Historically the station was often where passengers planned and booked tickets for their trip. Even a simple trip might involve detailed advance planning, especially on lines where service might only operate once or twice a day.

Long-distance trips were far more complicated, especially where two or more railroad companies were involved. Not only did schedules need to be consulted, but calculating the fares for tickets would involve a complex and time-consuming process. If journeys were taken overnight, reservations for sleeping car space or hotels needed to be secured in advance.

In the days when passengers traveled with heavy trunks, arrangements to ship their baggage were almost as complicated as the tickets, especially when changing trains. The ubiquitous baggage cart was necessary equipment at most stations, and baggage handlers were required to assist in the loading and unloading of trunks and heavy suitcases from the baggage car. This was typically carried ahead of the passenger cars toward the front of a passenger train.

When trains ran late, the station agent might receive updates over the telegraph and would report the arrival and departure of trains using his brass key and Morse code. Where stations were involved in operations, the agent-operator was often required to facilitate alterations to schedule as coordinated by a dispatcher. This was all accomplished by a thorough understanding of written rules and following detailed amending instructions issued via the telegraph. Morse code worked via a series of rapidly transmitted clicks representing letters as dots and dashes that were then transcribed onto paper by hand as quickly as they came over the wire. There were no automated SMS texts sent to passengers advising them of late or canceled trains!

Not every station had a telegraph office. In the winter when trains were delayed, passengers appreciated the station's potbelly stove fed by surplus locomotive coal as they patiently waited for the sound of a distant whistle announcing the arrival of their train.

The station was a gateway to transport. It was a jumping-off point and the place of arrival. It was an emotional focal point, where many people saw a city for

The former Philadelphia & Reading station at Tamaqua, Pennsylvania, decorated for Christmas in December 2014. *Brian Solomon*

Above: It was common for American railroads to identify their stations using the company insignia. Many railroads used the same icons for decades. Northern Pacific's was an adaptation of the Asian yin-yang seen on this North Dakota station. Northern Pacific adopted this symbol in part to reflect the importance of Asian trade to its business. Other railroads used regional icons. The Pennsylvania Railroad had its keystone, while the Lehigh Valley, Reading Company, and Illinois Central were among lines that embraced the diamond to reflect the importance of coal to their businesses. Central Railroad of New Jersey used a silhouette of the Statue of Liberty that could be viewed from its Jersey City terminal. *Brian Solomon*

Opposite: The Italianate style was commonly used for railway stations in America and around the world. Delaware, Lackawanna & Western's Broad Street Station in Newark, New Jersey, was designed by Frank J. Niles and completed in 1903. Today, it still hosts trains for NJ Transit, although at one time long-distance trains destined for Buffalo with through cars for Chicago stopped here. *Brian Solomon*

Above: This view of Toronto Union Station on an evening in June 2010 shows a clock and departure board, two of the standard features of most railway stations around the world. On this day, VIA Rail trains were operating as scheduled. *Brian Solomon*

the first time or hugged a loved one before they traveled afar or upon arrival after years away.

This book looks at many stations across the United States and abroad. By one estimate, when American railroads were in their golden age prior to World War I, there were some 80,000 railroad stations in the United States alone. Although a great many stations were subsequently closed and their buildings demolished, thousands survive and some continue to serve as built.

Many of the buildings pictured are in the Eastern states where railroads were the busiest. Here, overlapping and competing networks served America's busiest cities and most densely populated areas. For example, in 2015 there are more active railroad stations in the greater

Philadelphia area than the combined total of stations in many states in the far West (excluding California).

The size, styles, and continuing roles of stations remains greatly varied. It would be impossible in a book of this size to try to meaningfully feature every extant American station, let alone the tens of thousands of lost stations and the myriad of wonderful examples of stations in Britain, Continental Europe, and elsewhere. Instead, this book focuses on several of the most important precedent-setting stations—those buildings known for their great size, splendid architecture, or other significant features, while examining stations both large and small, past and present, in America and across the Pond.

1
THE GLORY OF THE
GREAT AMERICAN TERMINALS

IN THE DAYS BEFORE AUTOMOBILES and intercity highways and airlines, a big city railway passenger terminal was more than merely a station, it was the primary entrance for a city. In his 1916 book *Passenger Terminals and Trains,* author John A. Droege quoted Edward Hungerford: "The railroad terminal is the city gate."

Railroad companies reached their zenith between the 1880s and World War I. During that time, American railroads were among the largest and most powerful companies in the world. Railroads serving major metropolises such as Boston, New York, Philadelphia, and Chicago desired ostentatious displays of their wealth and power; building magnificent palace-like terminal stations was among the best ways to fill their desire.

Railroads were fiercely competitive businesses and often sought to outdo one another in the extravagances imbued in their terminals. Building immense classic

Above: Portland Union Station's clock tower is 150 feet tall, and its famous advertisement is considered among the city's most iconic landmarks. *Tom Kline*

Left: Historically, Portland, Oregon's Union Station served the Northern Pacific, Southern Pacific, and Union Pacific Railroads. Completed in 1896, the station's heavy Romanesque style and red-brick construction gives it more in common with its East Coast contemporaries than with many Western stations. Although not as busy as it was in its heyday, it still serves several Amtrak trains daily, including the Seattle–Los Angeles *Coast Starlight* and the Portland leg of the *Empire Builder* to Chicago. *Tom Kline*

15

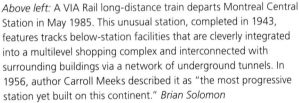

Above left: A VIA Rail long-distance train departs Montreal Central Station in May 1985. This unusual station, completed in 1943, features tracks below-station facilities that are cleverly integrated into a multilevel shopping complex and interconnected with surrounding buildings via a network of underground tunnels. In 1956, author Carroll Meeks described it as "the most progressive station yet built on this continent." *Brian Solomon*

Above right: The entrance of Canadian Pacific's Windsor Station in Montreal, Quebec, as seen in October 2004. *Brian Solomon*

structures helped railroads establish themselves in the image of the great empires. There was no coincidence that many major terminals were built to resemble the architectural wonders of the Roman Empire.

Railroad passenger traffic grew in leaps and bounds during the second-half of the nineteenth century as the nation itself grew. Immigrants flocked to North America, and industry flourished. Railroads attempted to cope with ever greater numbers of people on the move. But the

result was that a city station designed for traffic levels after the Civil War had become overwhelmed by the early 1880s, and the stations expanded during the 1880s and 1890s were starving for capacity by the early twentieth century. By that time, the well-established steam railroads were facing competition from new electric interurban railways, yet railroads continued to enjoy robust traffic, and growth was seen as a *fait accompli*.

In the early twentieth century, when railroads built their expansive new terminals, they could not have anticipated the effect that well-paved roads and widespread private automobiles would have on their traffic. Automobiles were seen as rich men's play things rather than mass transport. Stations such as New York's Grand Central Terminal were built for expected traffic levels much greater than existed at the time of their construction.

Ultimately the groundswell of traffic came, but it was not as expected. Although passenger traffic continued to grow after World War I, railroads were losing market

Boston's South Station's Atlantic Avenue façade reflects in puddles after a summer shower. The classic South Station terminal building was designed by Shepley, Rutan & Coolidge and constructed at the end of the nineteenth century. The building was threatened with total demolition in the early 1970s, but a compromise retained this classic façade, which was integrated into the modern station that serves both MBTA suburban services and Amtrak long-distance trains. *Brian Solomon*

		SOUTH STATION TRAIN INFORMATION			CURRENT TIME
Monday					
08-08-2011					4:00 PM
CARRIER	TIME	DESTINATION	TRAIN#	TRACK#	STATUS
MBTA	4:05 PM	STOUGHTON	917	4	NOW BOARDING
MBTA	4:05 PM	WORCESTER/UNION STATION	P519	2	NOW BOARDING
MBTA	4:20 PM	KINGSTON	043	TBD	ON TIME
MBTA	4:20 PM	FORGE PARK/495	717	TBD	ON TIME
MBTA	4:27 PM	FRAMINGHAM	P521	TBD	ON TIME
AMTRAK	4:30 PM	WASHINGTON, DC	2173	TBD	ON TIME
MBTA	4:35 PM	PROVIDENCE	813	TBD	ON TIME
MBTA	4:40 PM	MIDDLEBORO/LAKEVILLE	019	TBD	ON TIME
MBTA	4:40 PM	NEEDHAM HEIGHTS	621	TBD	ON TIME
MBTA	4:40 PM	NORWOOD CENTRAL	737	TBD	ON TIME
MBTA	4:50 PM	STOUGHTON	919	TBD	ON TIME
MBTA	4:52 PM	GREENBUSH	083	TBD	ON TIME
MBTA	5:00 PM	KINGSTON	045	TBD	ON TIME
MBTA	5:00 PM	READVILLE	763	TBD	ON TIME
MBTA	5:00 PM	WARWICK-TF GREEN AIRPORT	815	TBD	ON TIME
MBTA	5:00 PM	WORCESTER/UNION STATION	P523	TBD	ON TIME
MBTA	5:10 PM	FORGE PARK/495	719	TBD	ON TIME
		AMTRAK ARRIVALS			
AMTRAK	4:38 PM	WASHINGTON, DC	2160	TBD	ON TIME
AMTRAK	4:49 PM	RICHMOND, VA-STAPLES	86	TBD	ON TIME
AMTRAK	6:34 PM	RICHMOND, VA-MAIN ST.	ST174	TBD	ON TIME
AMTRAK	6:40 PM	WASHINGTON, DC	2164	TBD	ON TIME

South Station's train departure board. In the early twentieth century, Boston's South Station was the busiest in the world. While it no longer holds title to such an impressive statistic, it remains a busy railway terminal and served by hundreds of Amtrak and MBTA trains daily. *Brian Solomon*

share to other modes. However, because America itself continued to grow, and Americans became accustomed to ever greater mobility, it was difficult to immediately gauge the effects of new competition on trunk routes. But by the 1920s, traffic on rural branch lines was in trouble as new roads and autos really cut into the railroads' business.

However, it was the onset of the Great Depression that devastated railroad traffic levels. Long-haul passenger routes were especially hard hit. Creative means

such as faster schedules and new sexy streamlined trains helped railroads regain some long-distance traffic. Then, in the 1940s US involvement in World War II flooded the railroads with a record traffic tide. The largest terminals were finally pushed to near capacity, approaching their builders' anticipations from thirty years earlier.

For many years, Boston's South Station was America's busiest terminal. Droege gives it a special mention: "In the fiscal year ended June 30, 1913, [South Station] handled over 38,000,000 passengers, or 9,000,000 more than its nearest competitor, its sister station in Boston [Boston & Maine's North Station], and about 16,000,000 more than the Grand Central Terminal in New York, now the largest head station in the world."

New York's voracious population growth meant that it was only a matter of time before Grand Central outpaced the Boston terminals, yet the station never reached its hypothetical maximum. William D. Middleton in his book *Grand Central . . . the World's Greatest Railroad Terminal* (1977) wrote that this station was built to handle up to 100 million annual passengers. By 1929, it had reached 47 million a year. During World War II, traffic surged, and in 1946 it finally peaked at 63 million. But the age of heavy passenger railroad traffic was over. Despite postwar optimism that railroads could continue to serve as major passenger carriers, by the late 1940s the passenger business again started to decline and finally bottomed out in the 1980s.

TERMINALS AND YARDS

Big terminals consist of far more than just the passenger buildings. Complex networks of tracks are required for trains to reach the station, and safe control mechanisms are made possible by elaborate signaling schemes that ensure maximum capacity without risk of collision. In addition to passenger platform tracks, various supporting tracks and yards are necessary. This is especially true for long-distance trains, which require complete servicing and restocking between runs. Grand Central Terminal featured underground "loops," which circled around the back of the stub-end tracks, below platform level, for turning trains. By contrast, Pennsylvania Railroad's New York Penn Station benefited from similar turning loops (better known as balloon tracks) at its passenger yard at Sunnyside in Queens, New York. The following are profiles of some of America's great active terminal stations. Other terminal stations are covered in Chapters 3, 4, and 5.

The New Grand Central Station 42nd Street, New York

GRAND CENTRAL TERMINAL

Intended as a gateway to the nation's largest and most vital metropolis, Grand Central was built to awe the traveler with its tremendous size and splendor. A century later, it still stands and remains as a symbol to the former glory of one of America's greatest railroads.

The station's vast main concourse dwarfs the individual: three enormous windows face Park Avenue, while the concourse stretches nearly 300 feet with its great celestial ceiling. Here we have a railway station that depicts the heavens: illustrated by French painter Paul Helleu, the Zodiac above is a Mediterranean sky, but in reverse (except for the constellation Orion, which is as it appears in the night sky). The painting covers the whole ceiling and consists of 2,500 stars, of which 50 are electrically lit.

The station interior is dressed in a veneer of marble and simulated Caen stone, while its exterior is made from Bedford limestone and Stony Creek granite. The centerpiece of its great façade is a giant clock with an enormous sculpture featuring Mercury, Minerva, and Hercules. The great clock face perpetually reminds passengers and passers-by of the time. The station takes the modern commuter back to railroading's "golden age," when railroad travel reigned supreme.

Grand Central Terminal as it appeared in an architectural illustration at the time of its opening in 1913 when it handled 68,700 passengers on the average weekday. *Color postcard, Solomon collection*

Grand Central opened in 1913, anticipating the growing swell of passengers at a time when railroads had been enjoying sustained growth for decades without fear of real competition. But World War I changed the field of transport. While American railroads, including New York Central, continued to enjoy large passenger volumes through the 1920s, with the rise of the private automobile, railroads rapidly lost market share to highways. The loss of supremacy precipitated a slow decline in the industry, so New York Central gradually withered over the next half-century. Despite this decline, New York Central's core routes remained as passenger corridors. Its New York suburban routes, as well as those of the former New York, New Haven & Hartford, which also terminated at Grand Central, are still busy and have grown in recent years as regional highways have become clogged with traffic.

Yet back in the 1960s, the situation for the railroads was grim. In 1963, New York Central's longtime rival and potential merger partner demolished its equally

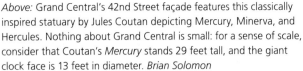

Above: Grand Central's 42nd Street façade features this classically inspired statuary by Jules Coutan depicting Mercury, Minerva, and Hercules. Nothing about Grand Central is small: for a sense of scale, consider that Coutan's *Mercury* stands 29 feet tall, and the giant clock face is 13 feet in diameter. *Brian Solomon*

Above right: Entrance ways to the platforms were dressed in stone and, like the concourse, exude elegance. The platforms themselves are entirely utilitarian, making for a great contrast. *Brian Solomon*

Opposite: Passengers line up to buy tickets for Metro-North's frequent suburban trains. Departure boards indicate the destination, track, and time of departure for each scheduled service. *Brian Solomon*

magnificent New York Pennsylvania Station, in what was decried as a gross act of corporate vandalism. New Yorkers were horrified, and Penn Station's destruction saved Grand Central from a similar fate. Legislation was passed to make it more difficult to destroy landmark buildings.

Today, Grand Central Terminal remains vital to New York City. On every level, Grand Central remains extraordinary. It's a supreme example of railway

architecture. Grand Central, like New York City, evolved over more than a century. Understanding the importance of the station requires a study of its history.

Looking Back to See Forward

Grand Central may be considered the ultimate execution of Beaux Arts architecture in America. Today's terminal, which was rededicated in October 1998 and celebrated its centenary in 2013, was the work of many people. Its vast size and design are a function of New York's urban parameters, of the strong personalities associated with the city itself, and of the New York Central Railroad, which facilitated the work of talented architects and artists.

Viewing Grand Central today, with its underground approaches and magnificent architecture in a setting dominated by skyscrapers and streets thronged with traffic, it can be difficult to appreciate that when the original station was located at this site in the 1860s, it was then on the *outskirts* of New York City. The station's name and location were established by New York Central founder Commodore Vanderbilt who consolidated the

main passenger facilities of his two New York railroads, the Hudson River Railroad and the New York & Harlem lines. This station also served as terminal facilities for New Haven Railroad, which was always a mere tenant to Vanderbilt's lines but which had a major impact on the terminal's eventual evolution.

Even in those days, New York was a difficult place to do business; Grand Central's northerly location on 42nd Street was the result of an 1859 law precluding the operation of steam locomotives further south. Even then, New York's residents objected to smoke and noise and were vocal in their opposition to locomotives soiling their city. So, though terminal operations were now relegated to the city's outskirts, Vanderbilt's new consolidated New York station was called "Grand Central Depot" anticipating its future centrality as the city continued

Grand Central's immense concourse as it looks now. Although the station opened in 1913, its design wasn't really fulfilled until 1998, when a large-scale interior restoration finally resulted in the installation of the marble staircases on the north side of the concourse (pictured) that mirror those on the south. *Brian Solomon*

to grow. The original structure, built between 1869 and 1871, was patterned after London's St. Pancras Station (see Chapter 5) in its use of an immense iron-and-glass, twelve-track-wide balloon-style shed, whereby the arched structure suspends the roof without the need for interior supports.

As Vanderbilt foresaw, New York grew rapidly after the Civil War; this resulted in overcrowding at Grand Central, so between 1885 and 1886, New York Central built a seven-track auxiliary train shed called the "the Annex." Growth continued, and in 1898 Grand Central was remodeled once again to accommodate trains and the swell of passenger volumes. The improved terminal was subsequently renamed "Grand Central Station." Although the name was short lived, many travelers erroneously continue to refer to New York's foremost terminal in this way.

The initial expansion wasn't good enough, so by 1900 New York Central decided that it needed a much bigger terminal. Based on its experience, it anticipated the need for further growth in coming years, yet it was running out of space to build. It was already handling an estimated

A Metro-North train disgorges its passengers into the fluorescent gloom of the upper level. Grand Central's platforms lack the neoclassic elegance that is characteristic of the rest of the station, perhaps an oversight on the part of its architects who failed to consider the importance of the boarding experience. *Brian Solomon*

500 scheduled weekday trains in its crowded station and congested open-air yards north of the terminal.

What to Do about the Smoke?

One of the difficulties facing New York Central was continued complaints about locomotive smoke. Efforts to curtail the smoke had been met with limited success. Locomotives were banished from the shed until departure time to reduce pollution under the copious span. Even so, the railroad was suffering from a dangerous accumulation of smoke in its Park Avenue tunnels, which at times was so thick that it obscured signals. Electrification was presented as a solution, and New York Central had considered electrifying as early as 1899.

Among other benefits, electrification offered a solution to congestion by allowing for construction of a two-level subterranean terminal while minimizing terminal turn-around time through the application of bi-directional suburban electric cars.

But electric technology was still very new and only in its developmental stages. While streetcar lines had been operating from electricity since the 1880s, and Baltimore & Ohio had recently electrified its Mt. Royal Tunnel operations in Baltimore to eliminate smoke from the tunnels, in 1900 there was no commercially viable technology available for intensive, heavy railroad operations.

Then, on January 8, 1902, a horrific accident forced New York Central's decision. An inbound New York Central train was approaching Grand Central; when it reached the smoke-filled Park Avenue tunnel, its engineer failed to see a stop signal and crashed at speed into the back of a stopped New Haven commuter crowded with passengers. Fifteen passengers died and dozens were injured.

This was the final straw to a sensitive problem. As is often the case, the media sensationalized the wreck, resulting in a massive public outcry. To quell public anger, New York City forced the railroad to eliminate its operation of smoky steam locomotives to Grand Central

The enormous growth in railroad ridership during the early years of the twentieth century encouraged Grand Central's architects to anticipate tremendous future growth, and consequentially they designed the new station to accommodate a tremendous passenger volume. *Brian Solomon*

by July 1, 1908, and this made the construction of a new terminal with electrified operations an immediate priority.

New York Central worked with top electrical experts and engineers to help pioneer heavy railroad electrification, while it planned for a massive new underground station. Considering the magnitude and complexity of the project, solutions were engineered exceptionally quickly.

Electrified rail service to Grand Central Station began on September 20, 1906, and by 1910, electrification extended beyond the New York Terminal 34 miles north (railroad timetable west) to Harmon (on the railroad's Hudson River mainline, and 24 miles northward to North White Plains on its Harlem line).

The new Grand Central Terminal building began to take shape in 1903 and required a decade to complete. Construction progressed slowly because the station needed to be fully operational the entire time, while arguments over the style of the architecture complicated its design.

Initially, Grand Central Terminal was to be the work of Minnesota architects Charles Reed and Allen H. Stem, who were well regarded for their railroad station designs but also blessed with family connections to key players in New York Central management. Later, architects Warren & Wetmore were brought in to aid in the design. Whitney Warren had been a student of the École des Beaux Arts in Paris and was a cousin to the New York Central's controlling family, the Vanderbilts.

On an operational level, Grand Central's engineers pioneered the use of a bilevel station and cleverly arranged reversing loop tracks (balloon tracks). Equally important was its architect's choice of gently sloping ramps in place of stairs to improve pedestrian traffic flow and using elevated roadways extending from Park Avenue around the station to make the building more accessible to road traffic.

Key to the station's success was the separation of the flow of suburban passengers from its long-distance travelers. As intended, suburban trains served the lower level, which kept the upper level free for long-distance and intercity trains. (Construction actually came to a halt after the financial panic of 1907, and when it resumed a while later, the plans changed radically for a much larger bilevel station than contemplated originally. Most notably, reversing balloon tracks were added on both levels instead of just the lower level for suburban trains, and provisions made for a separate lower-level arrival station for the New Haven that never was completed, although its tracks are used for maintenance and storage instead.)

To serve its passengers traveling both near and far, Grand Central Terminal offered a host of services and a variety of businesses within the station—a precursor to the modern, fully enclosed shopping mall. The station was integrated with the city around it, and numerous subterranean passageways connect nearby buildings as well as New York City's extensive rapid transit subway system.

Today, there are no longer any long-distance trains; these were moved to nearby Penn Station in the early 1990s. Both upper and lower levels host commuter trains, now operated by MTA's Metro-North. A new multilevel station is being planned *below* Grand Central to serve MTA's Long Island Rail Road.

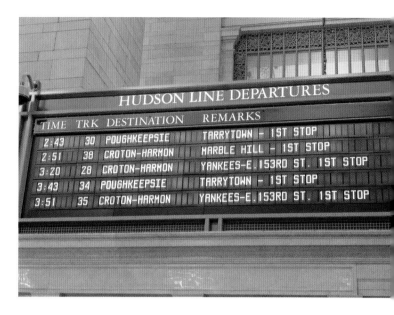

Above: Hudson line departure boards at Grand Central.
Brian Solomon

Below: Grand Central's architects and planners anticipated the need to develop the air rights above the terminal. The massive fifty-nine-story Pan-Am Building was built atop the station in 1964, more than a half-century after the station opened. The boxy modern skyscraper is a contrast to the eclectic Beaux Arts style of the railroad terminal and dwarfs even the massive *Hercules*.
Brian Solomon

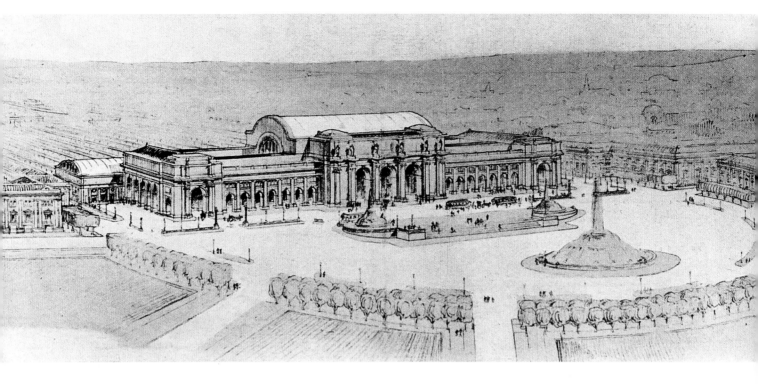

Above: This architectural sketch of Washington Union Station was published in *The Railroad Gazette* in 1903 at a time when the new terminal was being planned and was of intense public interest. The Railroad Gazette, *author's collection*

Opposite: Washington Union Station's destination board greets passengers with a list of departing trains, tracks, and times. *Brian Solomon*

Overleaf: In 2013, Washington Union Station was Amtrak's second-busiest terminal nationwide and accommodated more than five million paying passengers. In addition, it also served suburban trains operated by Maryland's MARC and the Virginia Railway Express. The station's impressive neoclassical façade was designed specifically for its role as the main terminal for the American capital. *Brian Solomon*

WASHINGTON (DC) UNION STATION

Few railroad projects produced a greater meeting of minds than the planning and construction of Washington Union Station. It is arguably one of the most significant twentieth-century railroad structures, both in its role as a railway station and through its influence on railway station design.

Planning for the station was a reaction to Washington, DC's, poor station facilities at the turn of the twentieth century. Pennsylvania Railroad (PRR) had inherited the old Baltimore & Potomac terminal located on the Capital Mall. While this station would have fascinated a modern-day railway enthusiast, in its day it was decried for its ugliness. In his book *The Pennsylvania Railroad, Volume 1* (2012), Albert Churella explains that

this inadequate facility was ripe for replacement, and by 1901, Daniel H. Burnham, one of America's leading architects, was already encouraging PRR president Alexander Cassatt to build a new joint station with Baltimore & Ohio in Washington.

The time was perfect for the construction of a classically designed palatial terminal. Cassatt was an influential polymath, a man of the Victorian-era and born of a wealthy family. He was blessed with an excellent education, good taste, and rare talent to make things happen. This was in the era before federal regulation interfered with the powers of the great railroads, and at that time PRR controlled the Baltimore & Ohio, its erstwhile competitor, and so there was no better time to encourage cooperation between the two railroads.

Architect Burnham was ideally suited to persuade men to make the necessary decisions that facilitated implementation of his vision for a world-class railway terminal. Author Carroll L. V. Meeks points out in his book *The Railroad Station: An Architectural History* (1956) "[t]hat it has been generally recognized that the World's Columbian Exposition in Chicago in 1893 marked a turning point in American architecture." He goes on to illustrate and criticize various interpretations of this sentiment but recognizes Burnham as one of the principal architects of the Exposition. Where the Exposition was little more than a temporary display,

Today, Washington Union Station's magnificent 96-foot high-barrel vault roof still makes for an impressive gateway for visitors to America's Capital. Yet, in the 1970s this iconic structure was a functional ruin and was in such poor shape that it was closed to the public in 1981 and considered for total demolition. Thankfully, it was restored instead and by the end of the decade had been reopened following a multi-million-dollar restoration. *Brian Solomon*

Burnham's later works were aimed at permanence; the buildings at the Exposition were made of plaster, while Union Station was made of brick, steel, and stone.

Churella explains that Burnham didn't rest on his reputation, but in pursuit of his vision he traveled to London to prevail upon Cassatt to move forward with the project. About the same time, the American Institute of Architects established a commission to prepare a general plan to "beautify" Washington, DC, and its parks. This group consisted of an all-star cast of influential American architects, including Charles F. McKim, Frederick Law Olmsted, and Augustus St. Gaudens, with Burnham as chairman.

Where difficulties in the construction of small-town stations and midsized city stations were comparatively light in regard to bureaucracy, getting the necessary permission for a massive new Washington, DC, terminal required

an act of Congress. In March 1903, *The Railroad Gazette* reported that Congress had authorized the PRR to occupy an enlarged site for its new union station. Soon the project was underway, and the October 16, 1903, *Railroad Gazette* announced that PRR had begun work on the terminal.

Like many large stations, this was a joint venture between architects and engineers. The station and surface environs were the domain of Burnham, who outlined his essential vision and then assigned execution of the project to his talented protégé, William Peirce Anderson, who had been educated at the École des Beaux Arts in Paris. (Anderson was later a partner in the architectural firm Graham, Anderson, Probst & White that succeeded Burnham and designed a number of significant railway stations.) The design of the necessary trackage and supporting infrastructure was overseen by PRR's chief engineer W. H. Brown and his counterparts at the Baltimore & Ohio (B&O).

Burnham and Anderson executed the passenger terminal in a neoclassical style but on a grand scale. *The Railway Gazette* reported, "The station faces directly toward the dome over the center of the halls of Congress, half mile distant, and will be treated in an architectural style in keeping with its character as the vestibule of the capital . . . the (station's) three entrance arches, 50 feet high, far exceed in scale their Roman prototypes."

The overall size of the building was awesome. Although much bigger than needed for the day-to-day requirements of Washington, DC, travelers, the station was built to accommodate the four-year highs during presidential inaugurations. The station was built with three primary sections: the main building with its waiting rooms, ticket counters, restaurants, and support businesses; the concourse; and, of course, passenger platforms and tracks.

The main station building has generally attracted the most attention. The general waiting room is covered by an impressive Roman barrel vault ceiling. The concourse, deemed the largest room in the world at the time of its construction, was 760 feet long and 130 feet wide and covered an estimated 97,500 square feet.

By design, most passengers using the station could avoid going up and down stairs, and the majority of the terminal was built on a level plane. Beyond the concourse are the tracks, 33 in total. Of these, twenty were stub-end tracks that were constructed at street level. The exception was access to the eleven remaining tracks depressed below street level. Washington Union was unusual in that it combined features of a classic city-stub end terminal with a through station, and six of the depressed tracks were designed to serve through long-distance trains to points south of Washington, operated by Atlantic Coast Line, Seaboard Air Line, Richmond Fredericksburg & Potomac, and Southern Railway. These six tracks funneled into a double-track tunnel that extended 4,900 feet below Capitol Hill. The remaining six tracks were initially reserved for mail traffic, with the provision that if traffic grew they could be easily converted to passenger use.

Washington Union Station was built and operated by the Washington Terminal Company, which was jointly owned by PRR and B&O. It opened on October 27, 1907.

In its heyday, Washington Union Station was among the most important stations in the country and served some of the best-known passenger trains in the East, including the B&O's *Capitol Limited* and *Royal Blue*, PRR's *Congressional,* Seaboard Air Line's *Orange Blossom Special* and *Silver Meteor,* and Southern Railway's *Crescent.* As with many big American stations, its importance diminished with the decline of long-distance passenger services after

On November 6, 1992, Washington Union Station catches the mid-morning sun. In the early twentieth century, architect Daniel H. Burnham designed the station building to consolidate older railroad facilities on the Capitol Mall and improve the appearance of Washington, DC. A decade earlier, Burnham had helped design buildings for Chicago's 1893 Columbian Exposition, and he incorporated similar architectural elements in his vision for Washington Union Station. *Brian Solomon*

CHICAGO UNION STATION: AN ELEGANT SURVIVOR by John Gruber

Chicago Union Station is a survivor—and an elegant one. It is the only intercity passenger station today in the nation's railroad center. Chicago, known as America's Railroad Capital, once had six mainline stations serving eastern and western railroads.

It is the third-busiest station in the United States, with more than 300 trains per weekday carrying about 120,000 arriving and departing passengers. Most use Metra commuter trains. The station is the hub for Amtrak's regional trains serving the Midwest as well as most of its overnight trains. Soon after Amtrak was established in 1971, it concentrated Chicago intercity operations at Union Station. Amtrak gained ownership of the station in 1984 and completed a major remodeling in 1992.

The concept for a union station in Chicago dates to the *1909 Plan of Chicago* prepared for the Commercial Club of Chicago by architect Daniel H. Burnham's firm, particularly Edward H. Bennett, who supervised, and W. Peirce Anderson, the lead designer. The published plan, with Burnham's imprimatur, emphasized Beaux Arts architecture.

Pennsylvania Railroad planned and designed Chicago Union Station, which was shared with co-owners Chicago, Burlington & Quincy and Milwaukee Road. PRR's flagship train was its famed exclusive overnight *Broadway Limited* between Chicago and New York City. It is seen here departing Union Station in June 1961. *Richard Jay Solomon*

It recommended a magnificent east-west corridor that would have passed through the Loop and over the Chicago River, leading to both a union station for many of the city's passenger lines—not only a few—and a massive public auditorium. The east-west plan inspired proposals until the 1950s, but was little realized.

When Chicago Union Station Company was incorporated in 1913, four railroads were involved: The Pennsylvania Railroad (through two subsidiary corporations), with 50 percent of the stock; the St. Paul and Burlington, each with 25 percent; and Chicago & Alton as a tenant. It took twelve years to plan and build and dedicate the station on July 25, 1925 (Burnham died in 1912). Mary Colter, the Santa Fe's southwestern architect, designed the Fred Harvey restaurants and shops in

The station. In the 1950s, Union Station emerged as hub for a variety of new streamlined trains, including Burlington's *Twin Zephyr*, Milwaukee Road's high-speed *Hiawatha* (running to Milwaukee and the Twin Cities), and after 1938, Pennsylvania's elegant re-equipped *Broadway Limited*. Traffic peaked during World War II. Yet some new postwar services were introduced, including Budd Domeliner *California Zephyr* that connected Chicago with San Francisco by way of Denver.

The structure retained its architectural integrity for many years. A major change, demolishing the concourse in 1969, made space available for a thirty-five-story office building. Now, more renovations are being planned to open up the Amtrak waiting area, a crowded space since the concourse was replaced. The Great Hall today is bright and sunlit, but not available as a passenger waiting area during special events.

Of all the surviving veteran employees of Chicago Union Station, Art Anderson of Downers Grove, Illinois, probably has the most information about the entire operation and its family of employees. He worked there first from 1968 to 1971, returned in 1979, and served as stationmaster from 1985 to 1988 just after Amtrak's purchase and takeover of station operation. Anderson remembers the sense of camaraderie, the pride in the workplace, the desire to provide the best possible service for travelers, and the cooperative efforts to get long-distance trains from both coasts into the station on time. It was all a part of the culture of the workplace and of the Chicago Union Station company. The employees had to satisfy the demands of four railroads for platform space and open tracks, as well as answer questions about buying tickets on competing routes like Chicago-to-Minneapolis without

favoritism. If the Pennsylvania wanted its *Broadway Limited* to move to its place at the station platforms at the same time as the Burlington wanted to move two sections of the *Denver Zephyr*, diplomacy was required since they could not move into the station at the same time.

For all its majesty, the station does not get covered very often. Alfons Weber showed "Picture Possibilities in the New Union Station of Chicago" in *Photo Era* in October 1925. Jack Delano made an extensive documentary of the station for the Farm Security Administration/Office of War Information in January and February 1943, covered in the Center for Railroad Photography & Art's exhibit at the Chicago History Museum and the book *Railroaders: Jack Delano's Homefront Photography* (2014) by John Gruber, et al. Gruber's, "Camera-Eye's View of Chicago Union Station" in *Trains*, August 1965, explored the structure's "aging dignity," a dignity that again will be a part of the Chicago railroad scene.

—*John Gruber*

Below left: Crowds of passengers move through Gate 22 at Chicago Union Station to board Gulf, Mobile & Ohio's *The Limited* for St. Louis in 1964. GM&O was a tenant, rather than owner, of the station. *John Gruber*

Below middle: The classic pillars and arches are an enduring symbol of Chicago Union Station. In 1964, a man walks next to the pillars, oblivious to the historic significance of the structure. *John Gruber*

Below right: Surrounded by space cleared for future high-rise buildings, the profile of the Chicago Union stands out against the night sky in 1964. A sign advertising the Fred Harvey restaurants hangs on the side of the concourse. Although the main station survives, the concourse was demolished in 1969. *John Gruber*

This period postcard view shows Los Angeles Union Passenger Terminal as it looked at the time of construction. In those days, it served primarily as a long-distance terminal for some of the West's most famous trains, including Santa Fe's *Chief, Super Chief, El Capitan,* and *Grand Canyon,* Southern Pacific's *Daylight* and *Sunset Limited,* and Union Pacific's *City of Los Angeles. Solomon collection*

World War II. However, Washington Union remained a busy station for Amtrak with its assumption of most long-distance services in 1971, and continued to serve Southern Railway, until it finally joined Amtrak in 1979.

The station architecture suffered from serious disrepair during the 1970s, and by 1981 the main building was closed to the public. It was considered for complete demolition, but instead was restored and reopened in 1988—eighty-one years after its original opening. Today, after a long period of decline and rejuvenation, Washington Union Station continues to serve as one of America's busiest railway stations. It is Amtrak's second-busiest terminal and located strategically at the end of electrified operations for the Northeast Corridor. In addition to Amtrak service, Washington Union Station also hosts growing suburban

rail traffic operated to the north and west by Maryland Area Regional Commuter (MARC) and south by Virginia Rail Express. Connections via the Washington Metro make the station even more useful to Washington-area commuters than it had been in the golden age.

LOS ANGELES UNION PASSENGER TERMINAL

Los Angeles Union Passenger Terminal (LAUPT) was completed in May 1939 and is often cited as the last large terminal built in the United States during the classic passenger train era. It is significant as a rare example of an Art Deco–era railway station and one of the few new stations that opened during the streamlined era. Its modern interpretation of the Spanish Mission–style design is largely attributed to the L.A.-based father-and-son architectural team of John and Donald Parkinson. Sadly, John Parkinson died in 1935 as planning for the new station was underway.

Arrangements for LAUPT were abnormally controversial, delaying construction. It was finally opened with an elaborate theatric railway pageant titled "Romance on the Rails" emulating successful events such as Edward Hungerford's "Pageant of the Iron Horse" held

Above: Los Angeles Union Passenger Terminal station, largely the design of Los Angeles architects John and Donald Parkinson, was completed in 1939 to host long-distance trains for Santa Fe, Southern Pacific, and Union Pacific railroads. In the 1990s, it was revitalized to host Metro-Link commuter rail services, as well as Amtrak California, and Amtrak long-distance services. *Brian Solomon*

Right: Los Angeles Union Station seen in the soft glow of evening. As intended by its architects, the station's approaches are flanked by rows of tall palm trees, making for an appropriate salute to California's premier long-distance railroad terminal. *Brian Solomon*

in Baltimore in 1927 and his "Railroads on Parade" at the 1939–40 New York World's Fair. Bill Bradley in his book *The Last of the Great Stations* (1989) estimated that the elaborate LAUPT celebration attracted a half-million visitors. Once the pageantry was finished, the station opened for business, and the very first train to arrive was Southern Pacific's *Imperial* on the morning of May 7, 1939.

Completion of LAUPT was well timed as America's imminent involvement in World War II would result in a swell of passenger traffic. Bailey explains that in its first year the station terminated thirty-three trains and originated an equal number daily. But during the height of wartime traffic this number rose to as many as 100 trains daily. In its early years, LAUPT served an estimated 7,000 daily passengers.

LAUPT is associated with the glamour years of American long-distance streamlined trains, and passengers had a choice of such famous trains as the

Santa Fe's *Super Chief,* Union Pacific's *City of Los Angeles,* and Southern Pacific's well-appointed *Daylights* and its overnight *Lark* that both ran via the Coast Line directly to San Francisco. Movie stars and celebrities would often arrive via first-class sleeping car to be greeted by paparazzi's flashes as they disembarked beneath LAUPT's station canopies.

Originally, the official name of the building was Los Angeles Union Passenger Terminal, but it is now Los Angeles Union Station, the initials LAUPT replaced by LAUS. While the importance of the station declined with the loss of most long-distance trains during the 1960s, the station was never closed or abandoned. However, by the mid-1970s, it was a shadow of its glory years.

Thanks to California's passenger rail renaissance that began in 1990, LAUS is again the most important station in the West. Where traditionally it was a long-distance terminal, today it is the primary hub for LA Metrolink suburban operations. Five Metrolink routes are focused on LAUS, as well as Amtrak's California's *Pacific Surfliner* (San Diego–LA–Santa Barbara) and long-distance services including the *Coast Daylight* (LA–Oakland–Seattle), *Southwest Chief* (LA–Chicago), and *Sunset Limited* (LA–New Orleans). Today an estimated 150 weekday trains, mostly commuter, serve the station, many more than even on the busiest days during World War II.

SAN DIEGO UNION STATION

When studying a modern map, San Diego would appear to be on a branch line from Los Angeles, yet it was the Atchison, Topeka & Santa Fe's (Santa Fe) original Pacific terminus. By 1885 the Santa Fe had built its route over California's Cajon Pass and reached the Pacific at San Diego by way of an inland line through Temecula Canyon. At that time, San Diego was a more important destination than Los Angeles. However, in 1887 flash floods destroyed Santa Fe's original line through Temecula Canyon. By that time it had reached Los Angeles and, in 1888, completed a safer route to San Diego via its LA trackage.

In preparation for the California-Pacific International Exposition of 1915–16, the Santa Fe erected an impressive new San Diego terminal. The exposition was held at Balboa Park in celebration of the opening of the Panama Canal, and in 2015 the park held a centennial celebration of the famous event. The Santa Fe's 1915 station was designed by John R. Bakweel and Arthur Brown, Jr. The building was necessary to accommodate unusually large crowds anticipated for the event. The building was constructed using a steel frame with brick and concrete, as well as stucco facing with tiled roof. The entrance was marked with a great archway flanked by Moorish towers, each of which display the Santa Fe's iconic logo arranged in colored tiles.

In its original configuration, the building featured a frontal open-air courtyard consistent with its Spanish Mission-style design, with arcades on the three sides covered by steeply pitched terra-cotta roofs. This was removed in the early 1950s to meet modern demands for a parking lot. Despite the loss of the courtyard, the Santa Fe's San Diego station survives as one of the best examples of extant Spanish-style depot architecture in California. Typical of the Santa Fe's big stations, it originally housed a Harvey House Restaurant. (Fred Harvey was synonymous with food on the Santa Fe, and

Above: San Diego's Santa Fe Station was also known as "Union Station." Although Santa Fe was the builder and principal user, until 1951 the station also hosted Southern Pacific subsidiary San Diego & Arizona (later called the San Diego & Arizona Eastern). Today it serves as the southern terminus for Amtrak California's *Pacific Surfliner* trains and Coaster suburban services and is a stop on the San Diego Trolley light-rail system. *Brian Solomon*

Opposite: San Diego's Santa Fe Station construction in 1915 coincided with the city's California-Pacific Exposition that celebrated the opening of the Panama Canal. Ironically, the canal siphoned valuable transcontinental freight traffic away from railroads. *Brian Solomon*

the railroad had a long tradition of so-called "Harvey House" restaurants along its lines.) Until 1951, San Diego was also connected by Southern Pacific subsidiary San Diego & Arizona Eastern.

San Diego was among the first California cities to enjoy a rail renaissance. In 1981 it rediscovered the virtues of electric streetcars and built a cost-effective rail-based transport system on lightly used freight lines, notably 16 miles on the San Diego & Arizona Eastern line toward the Mexican border at San Ysidro. The old Santa Fe station was restored in 1982 and now serves as a principal intermodal transportation node. The San Diego trolley stops in front, and Amtrak California operates San Diego–Los Angeles–Santa Barbara *Pacific Surfliner* trains.

Since February 1995, San Diego has served as the southern terminus for *Coaster* commuter trains from Oceanside operated by North County Transit District. These share the former Santa Fe Surf Line with Amtrak's *Pacific Surfliner* but make numerous local stops. Today *Coaster* is just one component of an integrated regional public transit system that includes the *Sprinter* trains between Oceanside and Escondido, as well as *Breeze* bus services.

TENS OF THOUSANDS OF SMALL STATIONS dotted American railways serving villages, towns, and small cities across the nation. Railroads have undergone continuous changes since the first lines opened in the 1830s. The businesses, routes, and communities along the lines have evolved. In the mid-nineteenth century, railroads emerged as the dominant form of transportation and retained a leading role into the early twentieth century. This was the golden age of American railroading and the period when most railroad stations were built. But what is a railway station?

In the golden age of railroading, a railroad station was the center of communication, by land and by wire. It was the primary gateway to and from town. It was a focal point for mail distribution, it was how packages and milk were delivered, as well as a center for commerce, news, and gossip. Often discussion of railroad stations focuses on the station buildings, yet in fact the "station" is really a location. The station *building*, often described in America as a "depot," may be included at the station but is not necessarily required. Further confusing matters is when old railroad station buildings are repurposed and no longer serve as intended. In modern times it is quite common to find old station buildings still adjacent to active railroad station platforms, but the building has been adapted for different uses and no longer serves as built. The blurring of the distinction between place and structure combined with frequent adaptive reuse of station structures has caused a variety of problems with station terminology.

A classic cast-iron station sign still identifies the Bellows Falls, Vermont, union station. Originally a Boston & Maine railroad building, this has been owned by Green Mountain Railroad (now a component of the Vermont Railway System) since 1988. *Brian Solomon*

Above: Bellows Falls, Vermont, is located at a strategically important junction. Historically, the north-south Connecticut River mainline (jointly served by Boston & Maine and Central Vermont) crossed Rutland Railroad's Bellows Falls to Rutland route and joined with B&M's Ashuelot line, which ran diagonally southeast via Keene, New Hampshire, to South Ashburnham, Massachusetts (where trains then continued onward to Boston). Today the station serves Amtrak's daily *Vermonter* (Washington, DC–St. Albans, Vermont) which uses the Connecticut River line as well as seasonal Green Mountain Railroad excursions operated by Vermont Rail System on its former Rutland trackage. *Brian Solomon*

Above: The old Western Rail Road (of Massachusetts) depot at West Brookfield dates from the late 1830s and is believed to be one of the oldest surviving railroad stations in the United States. It is located roughly midway between Worcester and Springfield and was a larger-than-normal station designed to serve as a railroad eatery. In its early days, it also served as a hub for stage lines to towns without railroad services. Western Rail Road merged with Boston & Worcester in 1867 to form the Boston & Albany. *Brian Solomon*

A railroad station primarily serves as the designated place where a railroad conducts its business. It typically serves as the place to board or disembark passenger trains and/or load and unload freight cars and may also serve a variety of operational functions. A station location may be defined in the railroad timetable and company literature by milepost and name. (Mileposts are typically measured from the main terminal or company headquarters.) Station improvements, including location signs, passenger platforms, protective awnings, station buildings, and sheds, as well as sidings, restaurants, hotels, and offices, should all be viewed as extras, and are not essential for a station to serve its most basic functions. Yet, often when an old station building ceases to function in its original purpose, it may still be clearly identified as a former railroad station. Classic railroad station buildings were purpose-built structures adjacent to the tracks.

Further complicating the identification of stations and station structures has been the evolving role of the railroad. Historically, private railroad companies owned

Above: Amtrak's former Boston & Maine station at Claremont Junction, New Hampshire, serves its daily Vermonter (Washington, DC–St. Albans, Vermont). A secondary B&M railway line once continued east to Concord. In later years this was operated by the Claremont & Concord Railway, a vestige of which still serves this rural junction. *Brian Solomon*

Below: In its heyday, White River Junction, Vermont, was a busy railroad town. The passenger station is relatively modern by New England standards. It was built in 1937 in red-brick colonial revival style and features an octagonal cupola atop the roof. Today it serves Amtrak passengers and seasonal Vermont Rail System excursions. *Brian Solomon*

and operated railroad lines, trains, and stations. During the second half of the twentieth century, most railroads ceased running their own passenger trains. Surviving passenger services were conveyed to a variety of quasi-governmental or government agency–operated third parties, such as Amtrak or various commuter lines.

In some instances, the railroads conveyed tracks, stations, and equipment to these new organizations, but often the passenger operator is merely a tenant on the owning railroad, which now primarily concerns itself in the movement of freight and maintenance of infrastructure. The specifics of each arrangement vary greatly, but the result is that often the role of the historic railroad station has changed, and this leads to further confusion in regards to terminology.

Above: The morning sun graces the former Baltimore & Ohio station at Washington, Pennsylvania. Railway stations typically use architectural styles that make them easily distinguished from other buildings; although no passenger train has called at Washington recently, there is no doubt that this stone-faced building (that dates from 1882) was once a gateway to the town. *Brian Solomon*

Opposite top: The former Pennsylvania Railroad station at Lancaster, Pennsylvania, continues to serve Amtrak's daily *Pennsylvanian* (New York–Philadelphia–Pittsburgh) and *Keystone* services (New York–Philadelphia–Harrisburg). *Brian Solomon*

Opposite bottom: The interior of Amtrak's station at Lancaster, Pennsylvania, displays a functional classical style typical of PRR's Main Line stations. Railroad stations tended to be solid well-built structures designed for lots of foot traffic. Heating buildings with tall ceilings wasn't a huge problem for PRR, which carried lots of coal on its lines. *Pat Yough*

In 2014, after years of neglect, the classic former Pennsylvania Railroad station at North Broad Street in Ridgway, Pennsylvania, has been nicely restored. *Pat Yough*

MISUSE OF TERMS

In America, unfortunate modern terms have been often applied as synonyms to *railroad station*. This has come about in part of a need to distinguish between active railroad platforms and repurposed station buildings, but also as the result of misapplied linguistic reductionism common in modern American parlance.

Part of the problem stems from the common misuse of the word *train* by the general media. In railroad literature, the term *train* is correctly used to describe a service, such as "the *Lake Shore Limited,* train number 448," or "the 10:15 departure from Union Station, train 174." The word should only be applied to rolling stock when that equipment is assigned to a specific service. Locomotives or cars stored out of service are not considered trains. Historically, the terms *railway* and *railroad* are the correct ways of referring to the mode of transport. The term *train station* is a corruption that has unfortunately fallen into common usage. It should be avoided in railroad literature for a number of reasons. For instance, because a station is the place where a railroad conducts its business, it is not limited to merely a place

Atlantic Coast Line's Orlando, Florida, station was designed by M. A. Griffith and built in 1927. It blends Spanish colonial architecture with Southwestern themes. Atlantic Coast Line merged with its rival Seaboard Air Line in 1967 to form Seaboard Coast Line (SCL). SCL conveyed its remaining passenger services to Amtrak in 1971. In its original configuration, it featured segregated waiting rooms, a characteristic common to many stations in the American South. *Brian Solomon*

Architect Frank P. Milburn designed this elegant Spanish Mission Revival–style station for Southern Railway at Salisbury, North Carolina. It was completed in 1908. *Brian Solomon*

The former Southern Railway station at Greensboro, North Carolina, was faithfully restored in 2005. It was designed by Fellheimer & Wagner, the architects responsible for some of the most famous stations of the 1920s. Built in 1927, Southern transferred ownership of the station to the city in 1979. In 2015, it served several daily Amtrak trains, including the *Crescent* (New York–Washington–Atlanta–New Orleans), *Carolinian* (New York–Washington–Charlotte, North Carolina), and a pair of Raleigh-to-Charlotte services run as the *Piedmont* that used distinctive equipment owned by North Carolina DOT. *Doug Riddell*

where trains pause for passengers. The term *train stop* is a further corruption; its application reveals a general ignorance of railroad history and operations and so should be vigorously avoided.

DEPOT VERSUS STATION

Another potential confusion may result from the differences between British and American terminology. This is by no means limited to railroad/railway stations, as there are a great many incongruities in the way that Americans, British, and the Commonwealth countries use the English language, notably in the spelling of common words. Railroad terminology involves a great many differences between American and British practices (*practice* is the term to cover the respective approaches to the technology and relates to spheres of influence that extend beyond national boundaries).

Some differences developed early, while others result from more recent language divergences. In American

A view of the old Missouri Pacific station in Little Rock, Arkansas, on October 13, 1993. Although it was planned as a Union Station, historically this composite Italianate structure only hosted Missouri Pacific passenger trains. Today the building is no longer railroad-owned. Most of its facilities have been converted for public enjoyment as museums, restaurants, and shops, while it continues to serve Amtrak's daily *Texas Eagle* on its run from Chicago to Antonio. *Tom Kline*

practice, the person at the throttle of a locomotive is called the *engineer* (short for *locomotive engineer*), while in British practice, this position is known as the *locomotive driver*. In America the engineer *runs* a locomotive; in Britain the driver *drives* the locomotive. The basic infrastructure has different terms as well. The wooden cross ties (or simply *ties*) on American railroads are called *sleepers* on British railways, while in America a sleeper is short for a *sleeping car*.

In modern American usage, a *railroad depot* is typically used to describe a station building and often

Above: The century-old former Texas & Pacific (T&P) station at Marshall, Texas—known locally as the "Texas & Pacific Depot"—is in the local historic district and hosts a railroad museum as well as an Amtrak station. It is unusual because it sits in the middle of a wye, a triangular arrangement where mainline tracks from three directions connect with each other. T&P was part of the Missouri Pacific (MP) system in its later years. Amtrak's *Texas Eagle* takes its name from MP's family of famous streamlined trains, and this serves the station using tracks now owned and operated by Union Pacific, the freight railroad that merged with MP in the 1980s. *Tom Kline*

Opposite: The board and batten-style station at Kent, Connecticut, dates from the early 1870s and was built to serve the original Housatonic Railroad, which ran though its namesake river valley and served a port on Long Island Sound at Bridgeport. Later part of the New Haven Railroad, this route last saw scheduled revenue passenger service in 1971. However, modern short line railroad has revived the Housatonic Railroad name and today serves freight customers between Pittsfield and the Danbury area. The old station is no longer served by the railroad. *Brian Solomon*

Above left: Amtrak's former New Haven Railroad station at Berlin, Connecticut, is small-town classic that has survived in both form and function. As of 2015, it hosts more than one dozen trains daily; inside is a classic waiting room and ticket agency. Soon, it may be transformed into a modern facility when the line between New Haven, Hartford, and Springfield, Massachusetts, is upgraded. Yet, will this classic building retain its rural charm? *Brian Solomon*

Above right: A detailed interior view of the Berlin, Connecticut, station waiting room stained-glass windows. *Brian Solomon*

infers a relatively modest facility. But this was not always true. Grand Central Depot referred to Vanderbilt's original terminal in Manhattan and was anything but modest. The hackneyed phrase "down at the depot" meant "at the railroad station." By contrast, in modern British parlance, the term *depot* refers to facilities where locomotives or rolling stock are stored or maintained between runs, and is thus distinguished clearly from passenger stations; in America these facilities were called either an *engine house* or *roundhouse* and today might be described as *shops* or *storage yards.*

CENTERS OF TRANSPORTATION AND COMMUNICATION

The railroad station was often one of the most important buildings in a town in the days before the advent of private automobiles and improved roads (let alone paved highways with a hard tarmac surface). Railroads served as the primary means for transportation and communication. A railroad official, typically a station agent, was in charge of the premises and often lived in the building in rooms upstairs, or nearby, depending on the specific arrangements

provided by the railroad. The size and arrangements of stations varied greatly but typically included a waiting room or two, a ticket office, toilets, and a baggage room. Larger stations may have also included express rooms and facilities for shipping packages and less-than-carload (LCL) merchandise; mailrooms for dispatching, collecting, and storing mail shipments from passing trains; a telegraph office; and railroad offices.

Where a railroad deemed that there was sufficient business, or at stations designed for the transfer of passengers between routes, including stations at junctions

The old Boston & Maine station at Ely, Vermont, is a well-preserved example of a rural country railroad depot and even retains its old train order signal. Decades have passed since this station regularly served passenger trains, and it was sold off by the B&M in the early 1960s. In 1945, two B&M local trains in each direction stopped at Ely six days a week with just a single round trip on Sundays.
Brian Solomon

Above: Not all railroad stations are old. New York City–based Metro-North Commuter Railroad began serving the new West Haven, Connecticut, station in August 2013. Conveniently located near Interstate 95, it offers commuters an ideal place to park and board trains for New York's Grand Central Terminal. The line also hosts Amtrak, but passengers need to change at either New Haven or Bridgeport for Amtrak services. On February 7, 2014, an eastward Amtrak *Acela Express* glides through West Haven on its way from Washington, DC, to Boston. *Richard J. Solomon*

Overleaf: The former Santa Fe station and Harvey House at Waynoka, Oklahoma, has seen better days. Sensing an opportunity, British-born entrepreneur Fred Harvey approached Santa Fe in 1876 with a proposal to improve their meal stops with a quality restaurant and first-rate staffing. His secret formula included not only high culinary standards but attractive, unmarried waitresses, known popularly as "Harvey Girls." The first of his "Harvey House" restaurants was located at Topeka, and his success with this enterprise led to him operating a chain of similar establishments along the railroad. At the time of this photo, the Santa Fe was still using the two buildings but later donated them to the city, which restored the 1910 structures to their original beauty. They now house a museum run by the Waynoka Historical Society. *Tom Kline*

Although less glamorous than passenger stations, freight stations provided a greater share of revenue for many American railroads. On some lines, freight and passenger stations were combined as a unified structure, while others used separate buildings. The former Santa Fe freight depot at Brenham, Texas, has been nicely restored and was once used as an Amtrak station. *Tom Kline*

and "union stations" served by trains from two or more railroads, space might be allocated for a variety of services, including newsstands, restaurants, and related facilities. In large towns or small cities, stations might be combined or built adjacent to hotels, which might be used by both railroad travelers and railroad employees.

The arrangement of these facilities tended to follow common patterns and conventions, but as Clarence Winchester explains in *Railway Wonders of the World* (1935), "The design of any station depends mainly on the requirements of its position and the convenience of the buildings both for the use of the railway staff and of the traveling public."

SERVICES, TRAINS, AND STATIONS

By the late nineteenth century, most American railroads scheduled at least two to three passenger trains in each direction daily to towns along mainlines. Heavy trunk routes, such as the Pennsylvania Railroad's Main Line

between Philadelphia and Pittsburgh, New York Central's Waterlevel Route from New York City to Buffalo, and New Haven's Shoreline between New York and Boston were much busier.

Most railroads operated various types of passenger trains, including mixed trains that carried local freight and passengers and operated on a loose schedule; all-stops local runs (often the so-called "milk runs") that ran on tightly timetabled schedules but at a leisurely pace; and express trains that skipped most stations and ran on expedited schedules, overtaking slower passenger trains and freights. Flagship trains carrying highly varnished, fine appointed, heavy Pullman Palace cars ran between major cities carrying first-class and "extra fare" passengers. These rarely stopped at small town depots. Even fancier were extra trains carrying the private cars of the super rich, influential businessmen, and railroad officers. These were the private jets of their day.

STATION NAMES

The name of a station was assigned by the owning railroad. In many instances, the station name neatly coincided with the common place name, and when it was convenient for both the railroad and the community, a station would be situated as closely as possible to the population center. However, it was not uncommon for a railroad station to be located a considerable distance from the town it served. This was often the case in mountainous terrain where it was impractical to build a line directly in an established village.

On the Boston & Albany, Middlefield Station was located several miles from Middlefield, Massachusetts, and at much lower elevation. Finding the site of this old station on maps today can prove elusive. While the tracks remain, the station and its buildings were demolished decades ago. Furthermore the station is nearest to the old village of Bancroft that was located across the river from the railroad.

A town or city would often benefit from more than one station. Multiple stations were necessary

Completed in 1908, the former Pennsylvania Railroad station at Wilmington, Delaware, was designed by Furness, Evans and Company and is one of many railroad stations in the region attributed to the brilliance of architect Frank Furness. It was restored in 1984 after decades of neglect, and today it serves Amtrak and SEPTA. *Brian Solomon*

when myriad population centers were located within one administrative area and it suited the railroad to make multiple stops. And towns enjoying more than one railroad company might find that each railroad would possibly build their own depot. In both cases, station names would need to be distinguished to avoid confusion. Wilmington, Delaware, for example, was served by mainlines of both Pennsylvania Railroad (PRR) and Baltimore & Ohio, each with their own station, and each was described by their respective railroad names—that is, "Pennsylvania Station" and "B&O Station."

This can lead to more confusion: "Pennsylvania Station" (when used locally) referred to the PRR depot and is not intended to infer the state of Pennsylvania as the destination for the passenger. So, in many places where the PRR operated distinct facilities from its competitors, its station was often so identified; Baltimore, Maryland; Newark, New Jersey; and Wilmington were among many cities where "Penn Station" referred to the PRR station. Yet, often when "Penn Station" is mentioned without qualification, it refers to New York City's famous terminal (described in Chapter 3).

Pennsylvania Station in Newark, New Jersey, is one of several "Penn Stations" along the North East Corridor. The term *Pennsylvania Station* was devised to distinguish Pennsylvania Railroad's facilities from those of its competitors. How many passengers over the years have accidentally found themselves in this waiting room instead of that in Manhattan? To the untrained ear the announcement "Newark Penn Station" sounds a lot like "New York Penn Station." The Art Deco masterpiece was designed by McKim, Mead & White, architects of many of PRR's finest buildings. *Brian Solomon*

Boston & Maine's East Kingston, New Hampshire, station is located 46 miles from Boston on the railroad's namesake route. In 1880, four scheduled passenger trains in each direction stopped here. This classic wooden two-story station is typical of B&M's functional passenger depots, where the station master and his family would have lived on the second floor. Like many stations, it played a role in operations, thus the need for the train order signal, which is now merely a historic decoration. Amtrak's *Downeaster* (Boston–Portland and Brunswick, Maine) service passes five times daily but doesn't stop. Although New Hampshire's railroads suffered early declines and there are now more abandoned lines than active railways, the state has dozens of surviving depots. *Brian Solomon*

STATIONS AND OPERATIONS

It was common for railroad stations to serve a key role in railroad operations. Passing sidings, either in conjunction with passenger platforms, or beyond the station buildings, were running tracks where trains could safely pass or overtake one another. On many American lines, operations were conducted using an established and highly regulated system of timetable and train order rules.

Employees' timetables were printed for the benefit of operating employees. Unlike public schedules, which are strictly advisory, employee timetables provided

FROST'S IMPRESSIVE STATIONS SERVE AS GATEWAYS by John Gruber

When railroad stations served as gateways to large and small communities, Midwestern railroads often turned to Charles S. Frost, alone or with partners, for designs for new, impressive passenger stations. Landscape plans for parks surrounding these stations, often the work of Annette E. McCrea, added to their civic stature.

Frost (1856–1931) received his professional training in the offices of leading Boston architects and by special studies at Massachusetts Institute of Technology. He moved to Chicago in 1881. He was a partner of Henry Ives Cobb from 1882 to 1889 and Alfred H. Granger from 1898 to 1910. Since both Frost, in 1885, and Granger, in 1893, married daughters of Marvin Hughitt, longtime president of the Chicago & North Western (C&NW), it would seem natural that they design stations along the C&NW tracks.

McCrea (1858–1928) had many Midwestern railroads as clients, including the C&NW and the Chicago, Milwaukee & St. Paul Railway (early on, often referred to as simply the "St. Paul," and since 1928, known as "the Milwaukee Road"). Postcards show the colorful parks. Her work is more difficult to pin down, but documentation exists for Wisconsin stations at Janesville (C&NW), West DePere (C&NW), and Wausau (Milwaukee Road).

Frost's first depot for the C&NW came at Oshkosh, Wisconsin, in 1884, and many more followed. "His work in this class of buildings has been very extensive, and reflects credit upon his reputation," according to *Industrial Chicago: The Building Interests*, published in 1891. When a representative of Frost and Granger arrived in Baraboo, Wisconsin, in 1901 to look over the site for a new passenger station and division office, the *Baraboo Republic* called the

Charles S. Frost designed the Milwaukee Road's station in Minneapolis. When the picture was taken in 1970, the *Morning Hiawatha* was the only train using the station. Today the historic structure and train shed have been preserved as a hotel and an ice rink. *Photos by John Gruber*

The design of small stations is very similar: each requires two waiting rooms, one ticket office, and a baggage-room, but so simple a problem, if considered rightfully, has many points important both to the company and the traveling public. It often makes a serious difference, in the economy of operation, whether the baggage-room is on one or the other end. The waiting-room should always command a view of the trains.

With the study of stations and his success on the North Western, his reputation spread among Midwestern railroads. Frost, alone or with partners, was responsible for plans for rival companies in Chicago; St. Paul, Minnesota; Minneapolis, Minnesota; and at least six Wisconsin cities: Beloit, Green Bay, Janesville, Madison, Watertown, and Wausau.

During a short period when the St. Paul was hiring an outside architect for its larger stations, it also turned to Frost. The *Beloit Daily News*, writing about the depot the St. Paul opened there in 1899, said: "It is a structure in which all

This is a fine structure provided with all modern conveniences, spacious waiting rooms, electric light, steam heat, etc.," the Wisconsin Railroad Commissioner's report said.

When the C&NW completed its station in Janesville, in a typical show of pride, the *Janesville Gazette* in 1898 praised McCrea's work to turn the surrounding property into a beautiful park. "The public should appreciate such improvements, for when completed it will make the Janesville station grounds the handsomest in the state."

At Green Bay, the St. Paul's passenger station on Washington Street was opened in 1899. When it closed in 1958, it was presented to the city and has been occupied by the Chamber of Commerce for many years. The North Western's station, opened later in 1899, had C&NW offices on the main floor until 1988 and served as corporate headquarters for the Fox River Valley Railroad through 1993. It reopened as a brew pub in 1996.

The St. Paul's station in Madison, the state capital, opened in 1903 and included a waiting room seating 200 to 300 people. The *Madison Democrat* described it as a monument "to the use and adornment of the succeeding generations." *Architectural Record* praised this and other stations in Wisconsin and Illinois as homelike, "the designer taking his cue rather from the surroundings of the building than from the railway and its functions."

Otto Kuhler, the industrial designer who styled the 1938 streamlined *Hiawatha* steam locomotive, also advised the St. Paul, by now known as the Milwaukee Road, on stations; a 1940 remodeling at Madison follows his suggestions. The building today is being reused.

The North Western's Madison station, delayed by objections to a proposed street crossing, opened in 1910. Division offices were moved there from Baraboo, Wisconsin, in 1933. It was sold to Madison Gas & Electric Company in 1965 for an operations center; a large office complex opened in 1983 preserves the passenger station and brick freight building designed by Frost in 1906.

In Watertown, Wisconsin, the St. Paul built a Frost station in 1896 on its mainline, less than a mile east of another station at the junction with the North Western; it has been gone for many years. The North Western's frame passenger station, near the junction, was built in 1904. It was last used as a freight agency in 1976 and is now a florist shop.

The North Western's Wausau, Wisconsin, station was opened about 1900. The building was "retired in place" by the railroad in 1963, the property sold in 1965. It has been used since then as a bus depot and restaurant. The St.

Paul's station, opened in 1902, became the focal point of the Employers Mutuals of Wausau (later Wausau Insurance Companies) trademark in 1954. The insurance company purchased it in 1977 and later transferred it to a Boy Scout Council. The company (part of Liberty Mutual since 1999) has a replica at its office along US Highway 51.

All the Wisconsin buildings survive today, except at Beloit, Janesville, and Watertown (Milwaukee Road).

In Chicago, they did plans for the LaSalle Street Station for the Rock Island and Lake Shore & Michigan Southern (New York Central), 1903, demolished in 1982; six suburban stations for the Chicago & Western Indiana; and a terminal station on Wells Street for the Metropolitan Elevated Railway, 1904. The C&NW buildings included its magnificent passenger terminal, 1911, demolished in 1984, plus suburban stations. Since Frost's main office was in Chicago, he also was responsible for many other structures there, including Navy Pier.

The Twin Cities work included the Chicago, Milwaukee, St. Paul, and Pacific Depot Freight House and Train Shed in Minneapolis, Minnesota, commonly known as the Milwaukee Road Station, built in 1897–99; and Great Northern Station, built in 1914, demolished in 1978, in Minneapolis. Although tracks to the Milwaukee Road station are gone, the building stands today; the adjoining train shed has national significance, according to the Historic American Engineering Record.

In St. Paul, Minnesota, architectural services included St. Paul Union Station, 1923; an office building for Great Northern President James J. Hill; Great Northern-Northern Pacific office building (since 1970, Burlington Northern); and Omaha Railway (a C&NW subsidiary) office building, 1917. For a time, Frost maintained a second office in St. Paul. Amtrak returned to the restored St. Paul station in 2014.

Frost was responsible for about 110 stations and 60 other buildings for the North Western from Michigan to South Dakota. He also designed Union Station in Omaha for the Union Pacific, 1899, replaced in 1931 by today's building, now the Western Heritage Center (see Chapter 4); Rock Island stations at Rock Island, Illinois, 1901, and Muscatine, Iowa, 1904; and standard plans for Nos. 1, 2, and 3 stations for the Wisconsin Central. He drew plans and received a commission for a new Bonaventure station for the Grand Trunk Railway in Montreal, but it was not built.

Frost's heritage is seen in the wide range of buildings for the C&NW. The work for other railroads adds to his stature as a significant regional architect. The many stations standing today, although not all in railroad use, are a tribute to his design ability.

—*John Gruber*

Built in 1872, the classic brick station at Chester, Vermont, has been beautifully restored and still occasionally hosts seasonal excursion trains. *Brian Solomon*

scheduled trains with their operating authority. Train orders were one way that railroad officials, typically train dispatchers, could amend, supersede, or supplement timetable authority in order to more efficiently regulate the movement of trains over the line and accommodate extra movements and operational aberrations.

It was necessary to have places along the line to distribute train orders to passing trains, and one of the most logical places was at existing passenger stations. Where no passenger station existed, railroads would equip a train order station or tower to do the work.

Dispatchers would issue orders via the telegraph, and line-side operators would copy the orders onto paper and deliver them to trains. Typically railroads issued two varieties of orders: Those that needed to be signed for by the train crew, and those that did not. Orders that required a signature restricted authority, and it was necessary to obtain a signature to ensure that the correct

operating men had received them. Orders that did not require a signature could be passed to trains "on the fly"—in other words, while the train was moving.

Having copied the orders, the operator would attach them with a string to a pole with a hoop on it and stand trackside for the trainmen to grab orders as the train passed at speed. Two sets of orders were handed to trains, one for the head end and one for the rear. Another distribution method used fixed line-side train order poles.

Stations where orders could be delivered were clearly marked on timetables, and each had a distinctive letter pair that identified the station to telegraph operators. Train order signals were used to indicate when a train needed to collect orders. A clear signal (vertical semaphore) indicated a train had no orders, a yellow

Opposite: Green Mountain Railroad's former Rutland Station at Chester, Vermont, has been a tourist attraction since the 1960s when the line hosted Steamtown excursions. A southbound freight approaches the classic structure in the winter of 2002. The old train order semaphores are now purely decorative since the traditional rules that mandated its operation were phased out decades ago. *Brian Solomon*

Above: On a rainy evening on October 14, 2005, the former Utica Union Station exudes a sedate classical style typical of many twentieth-century New York Central stations. Today, it serves Amtrak and seasonal Adirondack Scenic Railroad trains, both of which operate on former New York Central routes. *Brian Solomon*

Right: Utica is among the last former New York Central stations on the Water Level route in New York still served by Amtrak. Constructed in 1914, it was the work of what might be viewed as the transitional architectural partnership of Stem and Fellheimer and offers design continuity from the Beaux Arts designs by Reed and Stem in the early twentieth century to the classically inspired streamlined Art Deco masterpieces dreamed up by the Fellheimer & Wagner partnership in the 1920s and 1930s. *Brian Solomon*

The former Richmond, Fredericksburg & Potomac Railroad (RF&P) station on Railroad Avenue at Ashland dates from 1923, when it was built to replace a late-nineteenth century station swept away by fire. This handsome solid structure is credited to W. P. Lee. RF&P was a class 1 railroad with a busy double-track mainline connecting Richmond with Washington, DC. In addition to its own passenger trains, RF&P's route hosted through long-distance trains operating from Northeastern metropolises via the Pennsylvania Railroad to southern cities and resorts served by both the Atlantic Coast Line and Seaboard Air Line railroads. *Brian Solomon*

Although the station was closed to passengers between 1967 and the mid-1980s, today Ashland serves about a dozen Amtrak trains daily. The classic brick platform and three-bay covered porch provides passengers with a picturesque place to wait for trains. Unfortunately, the station building no longer hosts an active ticket office or waiting room; instead it's now the Ashland/Hanover Visitor Information Center. *Brian Solomon*

signal (diagonal semaphore) indicated a train needed to slow to take orders on the fly, and a red signal (horizontal semaphore) meant a train needed to stop and sign for orders. It was common to find these signals at small stations all across North America.

LARGE AND SMALL STATIONS

Railroad stations come in every size, from colossal city termini built on two or more levels with clock towers and office buildings reaching to heights hundreds of feet above rail level, to meager facilities, perhaps little more than a marker by the tracks.

The smallest and most lightly used local stations have been described as "flag-depots" or "flag-stations." Here trains are only scheduled to stop when a special signal is given, originally a flag, thus the colorful name. Author Walter G. Berg in his 1893 book *Buildings and Structures of American Railroads* notes that flag-stations "are frequently called second-, third-, or fourth-class passenger depots, according to the classification adopted by the railroad company." He goes on to elaborate that where there is both freight and passenger business, railroads often built a combined freight and passenger depot, but that in its simplest form, flag depots may consist of either an open or a covered platform or a simple shelter. Scheduled trains would be instructed to slow down and prepare to stop when approaching flag stations, but when neither a "flag" nor prospective passengers were visible, it could continue without stopping. Yet, on many railroads, flag depots still warranted significant structures, so historically the term didn't necessarily infer a bare platform without station building.

In later years, railroads looking to cut costs on lightly traveled lines would discontinue staffed station buildings at lightly traveled locations. While the old station building may have remained, possibly with an open waiting room, the facility no longer functioned as originally built. Amtrak still uses the term *flag stop* in its 2014 timetables. A pair of crossed flags are used to designate flag stops, which it defines as places where a

The restored former Buffalo, Rochester & Pittsburgh station at Dubois, Pennsylvania, as it appeared on December 26, 2014. The BR&P was acquired by Baltimore & Ohio in 1932. Today the station is privately owned, while the old BR&P tracks are operated by Genesee & Wyoming's Buffalo & Pittsburgh, a freight line created by when CSX sold the line in the mid-1980s. *Pat Yough*

This former Chicago, Burlington & Quincy station at Steward, Illinois, is typical of a small simple standard-plan structure that once served many Midwestern towns. It features a bay window that would have been facing the tracks when the station was active. Although this old station is still along the former Burlington (now BNSF Railway), it hasn't served as a railroad station in decades and has been relocated a short distance from the mainline. *Brian Solomon*

"train stops only when passengers are present, either on the train or station platform, and ticketed to and/ or from this station. Reservations are required." Often on Amtrak schedules, the "flag stop" is specific to the individual train, rather than being universal to all trains. Among modern-day Amtrak flag stops are Gastonia, North Carolina; Laurel and Picayune, Mississippi; Slidell, Louisiana, on its former Southern Railway *Crescent* route; Latrobe and Tyrone, Pennsylvania, on the *Pennsylvanian*; Thurmond, West Virginia, on the *Cardinal*; Essex, Montana, on the *Empire Builder*; and Lordsburg, New Mexico, on the *Sunset Limited*.

The former Burlington station at Stone Avenue, La Grange, Illinois, is one of two active stations in the town famous for its association with General Motors Electro-Motive Division. Purists will note with delight that EMD's plant is technically in nearby McCook but the builder's plates on diesels read "La Grange." This station, completed in 1901, emulates the design of a similar structure nearby on the Chicago & North Western line at Kenilworth, Illinois. *Tom Kline*

A common type of staffed small-town station was the "combination depot," which blended the functions of passenger and freight stations where neither business generated sufficient traffic to justify construction of separate station structures. Berg wrote in 1893:

> For the freight business a freight-room is required, with platform space along a wagon-road for transferring freight to and from wagons; and also the necessary platforms and facilities for handling freight to and from cars in freight trains or cars standing at the depot. A separate freight office is not needed, because at stations where combination depots are used the entire business at the station is generally in charge of one man, with one or more assistants at important points and the necessary clerical work, therefore is in one office, which serves as freight-office, ticket-office, and telegraph-office. This office should always have a projection on the track side, in the nature of a bay-window, so that the track is visible in both directions from inside the office. The passenger business is served by the introduction of waiting-rooms, either one general waiting-room or separate waiting-rooms for ladies and gentlemen.

Many major railroads assigned station design to the engineering department. It was common for individual railroads to develop a series of standard plans for different types of depot buildings. Although the precise arrangement might vary from location to location, the essential structural plan and space allocation remained more or less the same between buildings of the same class on a given railroad or railroad division. While on some railroads the buildings were intentionally styled with the intent of a family look to stations, on others it was common to vary exterior styling to suit communities along the line.

Berg offers a variety of detailed descriptions of various arrangements and sizes of existing plans for stations, including those of the combination variety:

> The combination depots of the Pennsylvania lines west of Pittsburg [sic], Southwest System, design by Mr. M.J. Becker, Chief Engineer, consist of three classes, respectively "A," "B" and "D," and are frame single-story structures, surrounded by low platforms on all sides, sheathed on the outside with vertical ornamental battened boarding and horizontal boarding, in panels, and roofed with slate. The walls of the offices and waiting-rooms are plastered. The foundations are stone piers. The platforms

along the face of the building are generally 16 ft. wide, reaching within 4 ft. 6in. of the centre [sic] of the track, and set 8 in. above the top of the rail . . .

He continues in detail:

> The building in class "A" is 40 ft. x 16 ft. divided into a waiting-room, 15 ft. x 15 ft.; a ticket and telegraph office, 8 ft. x 19 ft, including a square bay-window projection on the track side; and freight-room, 15 ft. x 15 ft.

The use of standard station plans and standard designs has continued into the modern era. Many 1980s-era Amtrak stations were built to a common plan and style, while commuter railroad stations often feature cookie-cutter prefabricated shelters.

ARCHITECTS AND STATIONS

In the late nineteenth century, American railroads, especially those in the eastern states, had become prosperous transportation empires. The educated, visionary leaders of these companies sought to enhance their image and offer communities along their lines a better class of railroad station, so they hired some of the nation's premier architects and architectural firms to design station buildings. In many instances, the social connections between railroad officials and prominent architects contributed to commissions.

Among the best examples of partnerships between well-known architects and railroads include: E. Francis Baldwin's designs for Baltimore & Ohio, Henry Hobson Richardson's work for Boston & Albany (and other New England lines; see Chapter 4), Frost & Granger's stations for Chicago & North Western and other Midwestern lines, and Philadelphia-based architect Frank Furness' designs for PRR and Philadelphia & Reading.

These stations, among the most elegant and iconic structures of the period, helped elevate the appreciation for the role of both the station and the railroad.

In 1964, Chicago Union Station train sheds were taken down for construction of a high-rise office tower. This made the Chicago & North Western Terminal visible to passengers. The elegant C&NW terminal was designed by Frost and Granger. Here is an ironic scene: passengers are getting on a Union Pacific streamliner that just a few years earlier would have been departing from the C&NW structure, but in the 1950s UP shifted its long-distance trains from C&NW to the parallel Milwaukee Road which served Union Station. Twenty years after this photo was taken, C&NW's terminal building succumbed to the wrecking ball to make way for more high-rise urban development. *John Gruber*

RAILROADS HAVE HAD TO COPE with continuous change from the time of their inception to the present. Changes to traffic levels, route structure, the size and capabilities of equipment, competition, and public expectations have been expressed in the alterations to stations and facilities along their lines. As demand for services has changed, railroads have made numerous changes to their facilities, including passenger stations along their lines.

The original wood-framed, all-purpose station house built when the railroad opened might have been deemed inadequate after a few decades. Either its facilities were too modest or its plain functional architecture was not up to the standards of a community that flourished following the arrival of the railroad. Perhaps by the 1880s or 1890s the railroad hired an architect and built a more substantial, better-constructed, and better-looking building. By this time, it was fashionable to surround the station with gardens and parks. Meanwhile, the old station may have been demolished or sold off and then moved elsewhere for another purpose. Towns and cities were proud of their new gateway. They often hired a commercial photographer to document construction or the opening of the building, and it might be featured on postcards, typically hand-tinted and typically printed in Germany.

Often a late-nineteenth-century station was deemed adequate, and it may have even served the railroad's

This scene at Oakdale, Massachusetts, was made circa 1903; here Boston & Maine's Central Massachusetts Branch crossed its Worcester, Nashua & Portland Division. Construction of the new Wachusett Reservoir in the valley traversed by the Central Mass required a significant line relocation. Shortly after this photo was taken, the new lines were put into operation and the station was relocated to the north along the W&NP line. Further change came in the 1930s when the Great Depression caused traffic on the Central Mass to plummet. The station lost its agent in 1932. The death knell for the route west of Oakdale came in the form of disastrous flood damage from the hurricane in 1938, by which time B&M had already ended through service. However, the old WN&P line survives to this day as a secondary freight route. *William Bullard, courtesy of Dennis LeBeau*

needs through the end of scheduled passenger service. Yet, in other situations, traffic growth or urban development may have demanded further replacements, and some railroads continued to build new stations into the 1950s.

The decline of passenger service beginning about the time of World War I gradually resulted in stations being downgraded and closed. To compensate for declining revenue at a lightly used country depot, a railroad might have first closed the agency there and relocated the agent elsewhere. In these situations, trains may have continued to stop at the station although it was no longer staffed. In others, passenger service might be discontinued and the station building reallocated for other railroad purposes or sold to a third party (see Chapter 4).

Old railroad station buildings, no longer needed for passengers, might languish for years, while in other situations, the railroad might desire the space on which the building sat for another application. Perhaps it needed parking for employees, or wished to expand its yard, or wanted to build an intermodal facility to load piggyback trailers or containers. If that was the case, out came the bulldozers to wipe the station and its history away.

Taxes on property vary from state to state and community to community. In states where old stations were highly taxed, railroads were quick to get the buildings off of their books. Sometimes even before

Above: This early-twentieth-century postcard shows the Boston & Albany station at Pittsfield with a local four-wheel electric trolley car out front. Before the advent of improved public highways, railways and trolleys offered the best and most efficient means of transportation. Both the old station and the trolley are long gone, yet Pittsfield is still served by Amtrak; once a day the *Lake Shore Limited* stops on its way between Boston and Chicago. *Period postcard, Solomon collection*

Opposite top: By 1914, Boston & Maine had absorbed many railroads across New England, included the north-south Connecticut River Railroad and the east-west Fitchburg route via the Hoosac Tunnel. Its station at Greenfield, Massachusetts was located near the junction of the two lines, a couple blocks from downtown. Today there is a railroad-themed park at this location. On December 29, 2014, passenger service returned to Greenfield, although trains now serve a utilitarian platform adjacent to the John W. Olver Transit Center that is located across the tracks from the former station location. *Period postcard, Solomon collection*

Opposite bottom: In the 1890s, the interurban electric railway was the latest in transportation. Lightly built lines were laid between urban centers, often using street trackage and side-of-the-road operations. Electric cars connected cities with smaller towns. The Midwest enjoyed some of the most intensive interurban electric development, and Indianapolis was an important interurban hub. This postcard view shows the famous Interurban terminal at Indianapolis about 1909. The large single-span iron train shed protected passengers while transferring between cars or walking into the terminal building. Most interurban terminals used simpler structures. *Period postcard, Solomon collection*

Boston and Main R. R. Station,
Greenfield, Mass.

Traction Terminal, Indianapolis, Ind.

Terminal Station in Atlanta was built in 1905 in a Spanish Colonial Revival style. It was operated by the Atlanta Terminal Company, and through World War II it was a busy place served by dozens of trains daily, hosting passenger trains operated by Atlanta & West Point, Central of Georgia, Seaboard Air Line, and Southern Railway. By the time the station was closed in 1970, only a handful of daily trains remained. The station was demolished in 1971. *Period postcard, Solomon collection*

Chicago's 1903-built LaSalle Street Station included an impressive twelve-story office building above its passenger facilities and benefited from above-street connections with the Chicago "L" rapid transit system. In its heyday, LaSalle Street was New York Central's western terminus and Rock Island's eastern terminus. Perhaps it was best known for *Twentieth Century Limited*, Central's famous train that ran express from Chicago to New York over the Water Level Route. The building was demolished in 1981. *Period postcard, Solomon collection*

passenger services ended, old stations were demolished to save the tax liability. In other places where freight traffic was very heavy, the risks and costs of maintaining line side structures encouraged railroads to sell, move, or demolish any unnecessary structures seen as being too close to the tracks.

Sometimes old station buildings survived for decades after they were last used by passengers. In some situations it might suit a railroad to convert a former passenger station into a maintenance depot. It was ironic when an architecturally significant structure, once deemed the finest in a town, suffered the indignity of

Boston & Maine's Central Massachusetts station at Coldbrook, Massachusetts, as it appeared in the early twentieth century. This route suffered from an early decline as traffic had already began to wane after World War I. Coldbrook was an early casualty, and the rural station was closed in August 1926. Although much of the Central Massachusetts route has been abandoned, a few of the old stations survive. The station at Hardwick, Massachusetts, is now occupied by a local pizza shop and, as of 2014, still retained its train order semaphore mast—equipment that has been out of use for almost eighty years. *William Bullard, courtesy of Dennis LeBeau*

having its windows boarded up, its clock tower denuded, and its platforms removed, while the maintenance-of-way department fills it with tools and supplies, or turns its old waiting room into a bare-basics canteen for employees. Then some night, when all the railroaders have gone home, vandals break in and torch the old building. Or a passing freight derails. Or, out of neglect, the roof starts to leak and after a few years the whole structure is little more than a ruin filled with rats, and the community only sees it as a hazard and demands that it be demolished. So the old depot is taken down.

Big city terminals are not exempt from destruction. In the golden age of railroading, as traffic swelled, railroads wouldn't hesitate to destroy a well-designed building built only twenty years earlier to make room for a newer, larger, and even more impressive structure. Such was the case with New York's Grand Central: The present Grand Central Terminal, now more than a century old, is the third terminal on the site. Later, as passenger services became unprofitable and less important to the community, railroads eyed their high-value downtown properties as ripe for development. By the 1950s, some railroads took on a "passengers be damned" attitude. If necessary,

passengers could be accommodated at Spartan functional facilities, while the grand gateway built in the golden years was demolished to make way for lucrative offices and sports arenas—or sold to the city to make room for a freeway, parking lot, or other modern infrastructure.

Philadelphia's Broad Street; Portland, Maine's, Union Station; New York City's once-elegant Pennsylvania Station; and San Francisco's 3rd & Townsend were among the stations that succumbed to wrecking balls when their owning railroads wanted the space for modern applications. Often the public, architecture aficionados, and railway enthusiasts were horrified and dismayed at such outward acts of corporate vandalism, especially where passenger services were still being used and passengers herded from historic elegance to sterile functional facilities. What had happened to corporate pride? To civic duty? How could railroads come to destroy their one-time city gift?

While many outstanding examples of railroad architecture were lost, sometimes the loss of one station helped preserve another. Following the loss of the Pennsylvania Railroad's New York Pennsylvania Station, legislation was enacted to protect historic buildings. The

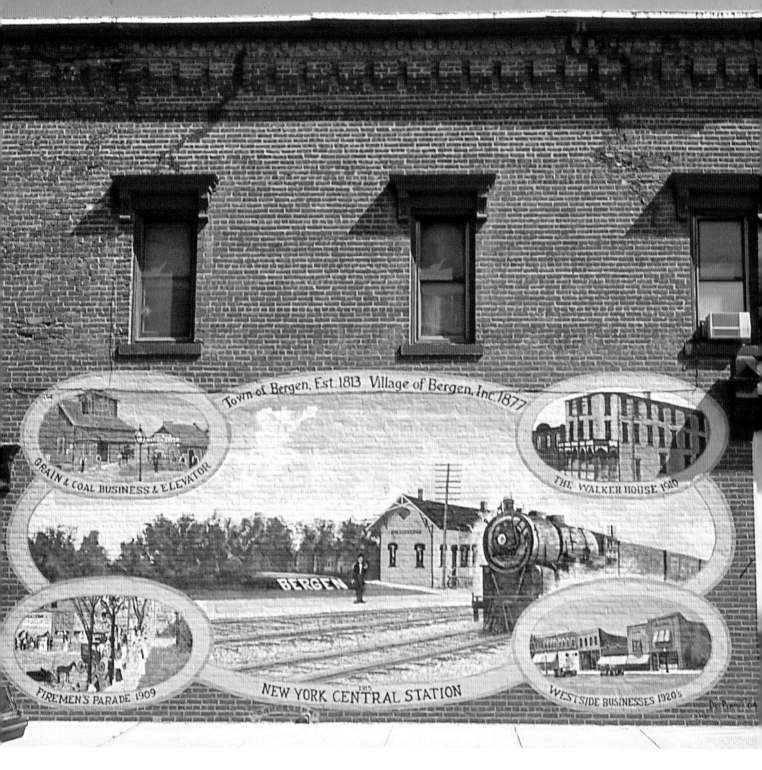

Town of Bergen, Est. 1813 Village of Bergen, Inc. 1877

GRAIN & COAL BUSINESS & ELEVATOR

THE WALKER HOUSE 1910

BERGEN

FIREMEN'S PARADE 1909

NEW YORK CENTRAL STATION

WESTSIDE BUSINESSES 1920's

Opposite: A Harriman-era 4-4-2 Atlantic type leads a passenger train paused beneath the wooden train shed at Southern Pacific's "broad gauge depot" (standard gauge, 4 feet 8.5 inch-track) in San Jose, California, probably before 1907. In 1887, Southern Pacific leased the South Pacific Coast, a fantastic narrow gauge system built between Dumbarton Point (on the lower portion of San Francisco Bay), Newark, San Jose, and Santa Cruz over the spine of the Santa Cruz mountains. Southern Pacific converted to standard gauge operations after the 1906 earthquake. *Period postcard, Solomon collection*

Above: Bergen, New York, is located roughly midway between Rochester and Batavia on the former New York Central "Water Level Route." Like many small communities along this heavily traveled railroad, Bergen lost its regular passenger service decades ago. Its station is recalled on this postcard-style mural painted on a brick building a block or so south from CSX's busy former New York Central line. *Brian Solomon*

In the golden age of railroads, elegant stations were routinely demolished to make way for bigger and better buildings. This view depicts New York Central's short-lived Grand Central Station, designed by Bradford L. Gilbert, as it would have appeared about 1900. This was destroyed to make way for the magnificent Grand Central Terminal that opened in 1913. *Period postcard, Solomon collection*

outcry and public disgust over the original Penn Station's demolition helped save Grand Central Terminal, which had been slated for a similar fate.

Yet, no station is ever safe. Nothing lasts forever. Natural and human-made disasters can strike with little warning. The enthusiasm that sees an old station restored can wane, and a new apathetic generation may not embrace or value history in the same way as their parents.

Photographs, memorabilia, and memories can help preserve lost stations. Often it isn't simply just the station that gets demolished. Railroads are abandoned or relocated and cities may completely redevelop old grounds. Where a station stood a century ago or even just a half-century ago may be unrecognizable today.

Take, for example, the old Worcester, Massachusetts, Union Station, a building that was replaced in 1912 when the new Union Station was built. The old grounds have been taken up by railroad yards, parking lots, and modern buildings. The old clock tower, which the railroad had made the effort to preserve because of its architectural significance, stood for another fifty years until it was in the way of Interstate 290 being built through the heart of Worcester. They called it "progress" and down came the old tower; today there is virtually no evidence of the nineteenth-century Romanesque Union Station that—in its day—was among the city's most recognizable buildings.

PORTLAND (MAINE) UNION STATION

In the 1880s, Maine Central and Boston & Maine were under common management and took the opportunity to consolidate several older facilities at Portland, Maine, into a unified terminal called Portland Union Station—not to be confused with a structure of the same name in Portland, Oregon. This was intended as an architectural monument; its American Medieval style mixed a variety of architectural styles and included Moorish and Methodist elements. The station building was designed by Boston architects Bradlee, Winslow & Witherel and built by J. Cunningham.

The impressive new station opened on June 25, 1888. Typical of the period, it consisted of a head house with a train shed behind. The head house was constructed from New England Redstone and pink granite. Its distinctive clock tower soon became a Portland icon. The business

Opposite: Boston & Maine's famous class P4a Pacific 3713 departs Portland Union Station with the *East Wind* on the first leg of its trip to Washington, DC, on August 8, 1940. The *East Wind* was a seasonal train introduced in June 1940 and operated jointly by B&M, New Haven, and Pennsylvania Railroads. Although Portland Union Station was demolished, B&M 3713 survives. It was displayed outside of the Boston Museum of Science for years and is undergoing restoration at Steamtown in Scranton, Pennsylvania. *George C. Corey*

The Union Station at Portland, Maine, was located near the intersection of St. John Street and Park Avenue. The Romanesque building was among the last buildings designed by Boston architects Bradlee, Winslow & Wetherill. It was built in 1888 when Boston & Maine and Maine Central were under common control. Destruction of the station in 1961 seemed to symbolize the end of traditional railroad passenger services to Maine, although Boston & Maine continued operate its Boston–Portland trains for a few more years. In 2001, after a hiatus of more than 30 years, Amtrak's *Downeaster* service restored Portland to the American passenger map. *Period postcard, Solomon collection*

end of the station consisted of a four-track iron train shed covering four tracks.

By the late 1950s, passenger services to Maine were in rapid decline, and in 1960, following Labor Day, the Maine Central discontinued all remaining scheduled trains, making it among the first large railroads in the East to be freight only. Although Boston & Maine services continued for a few more years, in July 1961, the old terminal building and its train shed were demolished to make room for a shopping center.

The station's violent demolition sent shockwaves across the country. It signaled the end of an era. Here the

loss of the station seemed symbolic of the end of the passenger train. Images of the elegant clock tower collapsing in a cloud of dust made front-page news. While the narrow-minded heralded the station's destruction as the march of progress, many others were saddened by the loss of the historic building. In many instances, Portland Union proved the martyr and, undoubtedly, helped foster station preservation movements across North America.

EAST BROOKFIELD (MASSACHUSETTS) STATION

East Brookfield, Massachusetts' Boston & Albany Railroad station, was among twenty-three stations designed by architects Shepley, Rutan, and Coolidge in the Richardson Romanesque style (see Chapter 4). Although it hadn't been a regular passenger station in more than fifty years, the station had been in use by CSX Transportation as an operations base and storage facility for its signaling department. CSX inherited the station when it assumed operations on the old Boston & Albany route from Conrail in spring 1999. While the condition of the station had languished since its heyday, the station had just benefited from a new slate roof when it was maliciously destroyed by an arsonist in September 2010. A local preservation effort tried to save the remains of the historic building that had once been an important part of the town. Unfortunately, they were too late, and in the end the remains of the station were bulldozed into oblivion. The East Brookfield depot, like so many American stations, was erased from the scene. All that remain are photos and memories. A large print of the old station hangs on the wall of East Brookfield Pizza on Route 9, just a few blocks from where the old station stood.

NEW YORK CITY'S PENNSYLVANIA STATION

Today, Pennsylvania Station is one of America's busiest terminals, serving trains for Amtrak, Long Island Rail

Road, and NJ Transit. In 2013 it was Amtrak's busiest station by a long margin, with nearly 9.6 million passengers using it. How can a station this busy be considered lost?

While the station survives, its great architecture is but a memory. Thus, Pennsylvania Station offers one of the best illustrations of the difference between a railroad

Looking west at East Brookfield, Massachusetts, on October 25, 2009. The old Boston & Albany station was a vestige of the era when the railroad served every small town along its mainline. It had been a half-century since the last train stopped here, and even then it was a carry over to an earlier time. In its heyday, East Brookfield was the junction between B&A's North Brookfield Branch and the mainline. A branch train made as many as nine trips daily to meet through mainline trains. The station was torched by a suspected arsonist less than a year after this photo was exposed.
Brian Solomon

station as distinguished from its station *buildings*. In many other circumstances, station buildings survive but no longer function as intended; in Penn Station's case the situation is just the opposite.

In the early 1960s, Pennsylvania Railroad cannibalized its crown jewel—demolishing the wondrous architecture it had built as demonstration of its Imperial power and its gift to New York—in order to profit from development of the site. This gross act of corporate vandalism was enormously controversial in its day. The destruction of Pennsylvania Station's terminal building—considered the greatest of all American stations—is one of the great tragedies stemming from the decline of America's railroads.

At the beginning of the twentieth century, PRR President Alexander Cassatt was inspired by a visit to the recently opened Gare du Quai d'Orsay in Paris. This revolutionary station design featured electrically powered trains that came directly into the station building. Cassatt's vision for Pennsylvania Station in Manhattan was to bring electric trains through deep tunnels below the Hudson and East Rivers directly to Manhattan Island. It was one of the most ambitious railroad projects ever conceived and sought to rectify PRR's inadequate New York terminal situation.

It had seemed intolerable to Cassatt that PRR's archrival, Vanderbilt's New York Central & Hudson River Railroad, served Manhattan directly, while PRR's own passengers arrived at a waterfront terminal in Jersey City and transferred to New York–bound ferries. And, to facilitate this cross-Hudson traffic, PRR built an immense glass and steel arched train shed in 1891—deemed the largest such shed in the world at the time.

Following Cassatt's return to the United States from Europe, PRR hired McKim, Mead & White—one of the best-known architectural firms in New York City—to design the terminal. Charles McKim had been a student of H. H. Richardson (see Chapter 4) and was well schooled in classic architectural design, but more importantly he was a personal friend of Cassatt, and both men shared an appreciation for classical European

A rare previously unpublished view of New York Pennsylvania Station viewed from the 7th Avenue entrance shortly before the legendary station building was closed and demolished in 1963. McKim, Mead & White's Beaux Arts masterpiece was partially patterned on the famous Baths of Caracalla in Rome. *Richard Jay Solomon*

culture. So when McKim suggested a grand station building patterned after the Baths of Caracalla and the Basilica of Constantine in Rome, Cassatt was delighted, and the work soon commenced though it took nearly a decade to complete.

The terminal building was enormous and featured tall marble columns with vast open spaces. Sculptor Adolph A. Weinman had decorated the terminal with giant stone eagles, ancient symbols of imperial power. New York's Pennsylvania Station was no mere depot—it was a monument to the Pennsylvania Railroad and to New York City. It opened for business in 1910.

The entire structure occupied two city blocks, more than 7.5 acres of land. The *New York Times* described it as the "largest and handsomest in the world." A tremendous vaulted ceiling in the waiting room rose 150 feet above the floor, supported by eight huge Corinthian columns. The main waiting room in Penn Station was fashioned from Travertine marble imported from Italy. The waiting room's vast interior space was dwarfed by the station's concourse and courtyard. This portion of the structure was built with granite and featured a complex structure of steel latticework columns and arches. Immense glass skylights illuminated the tremendous space, with shafts of light streaming down from the ceiling, creating a surreal atmosphere.

Yet the business end of the station was more than 40 feet below street level, where twenty-one tracks served passenger trains. To the east were four East River tunnels, to the west a pair of Hudson River tunnels—among them there were approximately 1,000 rail moves daily, all of which were protected by one of the earliest automatic block-signaling systems to use modern colored light signals.

Sadly, neither of the two men most responsible for the station's creation lived to see it. Cassatt died at age sixty-seven from heart failure on December 28, 1906. McKim died less than two years later.

Penn Station blossomed with traffic during the first half of the twentieth century. The high-water mark came

Amtrak AEM-7 electric 906 negotiates ladder tracks at New York Pennsylvania Station in August 1994. Although the magnificent architecture was destroyed in 1963, Penn Station remains one of America's busiest railway stations. Platforms and tracks are entirely below street level while space above the station has been developed for offices and the famous Madison Square Garden arena. *Richard Jay Solomon*

during World War II. After the war, suburban growth sustained intensive commuter traffic on the Long Island Rail Road and Pennsylvania's own lines, while long-distance traffic to Boston and Washington remained comparatively robust, both of which kept the station relatively busy despite general declines elsewhere.

During the war, the great glass ceiling was painted over because of a fear of air raids, and after the war, the station building was allowed to deteriorate. It lost its imperial elegance and became tatty, which unfortunately reflected the declining condition of the PRR. Although the company remained America's largest railroad, its finances were in tatters, and by the early 1960s, it was suffering enormous losses. It viewed Penn Station as valuable real estate and opted to replace the once-opulent station building with something that would generate more revenue.

Despite a public outcry and efforts to save it, Pennsylvania Station's glorious architecture was demolished in 1963 and replaced with functional structures lacking the inspiration and style of the original building. Today, the 1960s-era Madison Square Garden occupies the space above Pennsylvania Station. The old buildings have been gone for nearly as long as they stood.

PHILADELPHIA'S BROAD STREET STATION

Pennsylvania Railroad's company headquarters and busiest station was in Philadelphia. Here, in 1881, the railroad built its most impressive building, strategically located across from City Hall. To approach the station, its tracks crossed the Schuylkill River and reached Center City on a solid, multiple-track, elevated structure along Filbert Street that became universally known as "the Chinese Wall" (an allusion to the Great Wall of China). The wall, despite being necessary to get trains to the terminal, annoyed prominent Philadelphians who for the next seventy years would badger the PRR to have it removed.

PRR's original Broad Street terminal building was built in the then-popular Gothic Revival style—PRR's answer to London's magnificent St. Pancras terminal. A swell of traffic in the station's first decade led PRR to expand the facility in the early 1890s, hiring prominent Philadelphia architect Frank Furness to style the addition consistent with the existing structure. Built on the south side of the original station, Furness' High Victorian

Gothic head house, the principal station building located immediately beyond the stub-end trackage arrangement, thus positioned at the "head of the station," became a Philadelphia icon, and arguably the finest such head house built in North America during the Victorian era. At the time, PRR was vying for regional supremacy with Philadelphia & Reading, which was simultaneously building its Reading Terminal facing Market Street a few blocks to the east. The 1890s expansion included construction of a vast balloon shed over the top of the existing shed, which then was consequently removed.

Broad Street endured a long decline, partially as a function of its stub-end design and its central location (see Chapter 1) that was ill-suited to PRR's operation of through long-distance trains. The beginning of the end came in the early morning of June 11, 1923, when a fire badly damaged the train shed and station. Although the railroad swiftly rebuilt the terminal, the shed had to be dismantled. Between 1928 and 1933, the construction of Suburban Station and the new through station at 30th Street doomed Broad Street. Yet, Broad Street endured until the early 1950s, partially because GG1 electric passenger locomotives were ill-suited for service into the new Suburban Station.

Finally on April 27, 1952, Broad Street was closed and the station building demolished shortly thereafter. At the time, PRR President James Symes issued a public statement saying, "It is an old landmark that many of us will dislike seeing go: but *remember*—it is being replaced with Pennsylvania Station at 30th Street, one of the most modern, practical, and beautiful passenger terminals in the world—barring none." Yet, a decade later, Symes' philosophy—or historical ambivalence—resulted in demolition of another of the railroad's landmark stations: Pennsylvania Station in New York City.

Opposite above: In its heyday, Philadelphia Broad Street Station was among the finest examples of a stub-end terminal with magnificent head house and balloon shed. It was patterned after London's St. Pancras Station. This view was made from one of the signal towers after the 1890s expansion. This large shed was built over the top of its predecessor (which was then dismantled). *Period postcard, Sean Solomon collection*

Opposite below: Furness's High Victorian Gothic Broad Street Station head house was a Philadelphia icon. It was demolished in the early 1950s. *Period postcard, Sean Solomon collection*

Broad St. Station from Switch Tower, Philadelphia, Pa.

Broad St. Station, Philadelphia, Pa.

4 GLORY, DECLINE, AND REBIRTH

AS PRIVATE RAILROADS BEGAN TO SCALE BACK their passenger services, a process that began on some lines as early as the 1920s and became a national trend after World War II, the role of the passenger station changed. In some situations railroads continued to use stations after passenger service was discontinued.

Station buildings that housed offices, crew rooms, control towers, and dispatchers and served as maintenance depots remained important to the companies that owned them.

However, as railroading declined and evolved, and railroad companies began their feverish pace of merger, consolidation, and abandonment from the late 1960s onward, the role of many stations changed.

In many places, the large stations that had served railroads in non-passenger capacities were no longer needed at all. In their efforts to scale back costs and achieve ever-greater efficiency, railroads greatly reduced the size of their workforces. Improved employee productivity—made possible by new technology including computers, better communications, more powerful locomotives, and revised work rules—left many railroad buildings empty.

Old stations, devoid of passengers and railroaders, were sometimes allowed to decay in place. The once elegant city gateway gradually rotted, became an eyesore, and deteriorated into a sad reminder of the once-important role played by the railroad. While in some

By the time of this October 2004 photograph, the old Boston & Maine station at Eagle Bridge, New York, had long outlived its usefulness. The mast for its train order signal has been shorn of semaphore blades, its days as a communication and transportation hub having passed decades earlier. Yet, Eagle Bridge itself survives as a railroad junction where Battenkill Railroad interchanges freight with Pan Am Southern and Canadian Pacific. Many old station buildings like this one linger, waiting to be transformed or destroyed. What will become of the station at Eagle Bridge and its kin? *Brian Solomon*

Above: Imagine a time when a handsome hand-polished 4-4-0 American-type steam locomotive led a three- or four-car train of varnished wooden passenger cars at this Boston & Maine station in Ossipee, New Hamphire. Today, the old station is a forlorn ruin, a reminder of another era. Nature is gradually reclaiming the right of way as well as the building itself. It's just one of many surviving station buildings in the United States that has outlived its original purpose. *Tim Doherty*

Opposite top: An October 2001 sunrise greets the former Delaware, Lackawanna & Western station at Binghamton, New York. In its heyday this was a calling point for the railroad's famous *Lackawanna Limited,* a train advertised as "the route of Phoebe Snow"—a fictional character dreamed up to promote the use of clean-burning anthracite coal and DL&W's route between Hoboken and Buffalo. DL&W merged with its rival, Erie Railroad, to form Erie-Lackawanna in 1960 and Erie-Lackawanna discontinued its long-distance passenger services prior to the formation of Amtrak in 1971. Today, although Binghamton remains as an important rail-center, it hasn't had passenger service in forty-five years. *Brian Solomon*

Opposite bottom: The old Erie Railroad station at Silver Spring, New York, has tracks on both sides of the building. Erie's Hornell–Buffalo mainline is on the west side, while a vestige of the Buffalo, Rochester & Pittsburgh branch to Perry, New York, runs on the east side. Although passenger service was discontinued decades ago, the building has survived as a railroad-owned structure and continued to serve as a train order office into the mid-1980s. This sunrise view was exposed on a quiet morning in 2005. *Brian Solomon*

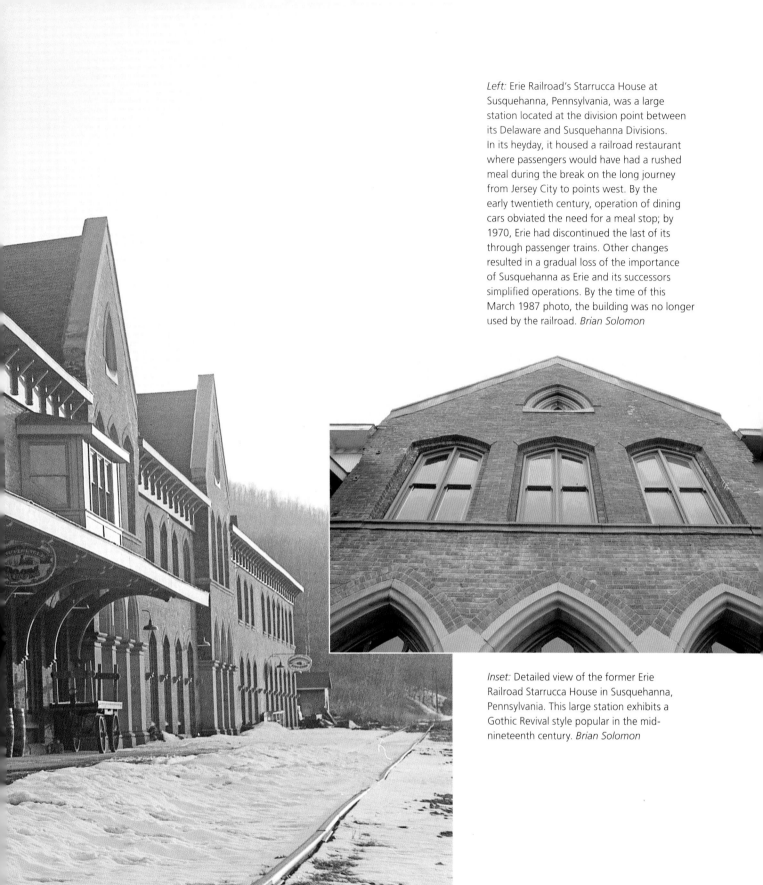

Left: Erie Railroad's Starrucca House at Susquehanna, Pennsylvania, was a large station located at the division point between its Delaware and Susquehanna Divisions. In its heyday, it housed a railroad restaurant where passengers would have had a rushed meal during the break on the long journey from Jersey City to points west. By the early twentieth century, operation of dining cars obviated the need for a meal stop; by 1970, Erie had discontinued the last of its through passenger trains. Other changes resulted in a gradual loss of the importance of Susquehanna as Erie and its successors simplified operations. By the time of this March 1987 photo, the building was no longer used by the railroad. *Brian Solomon*

Inset: Detailed view of the former Erie Railroad Starrucca House in Susquehanna, Pennsylvania. This large station exhibits a Gothic Revival style popular in the midnineteenth century. *Brian Solomon*

Above: Often the role of the station building has been divorced from its original function despite adjacent platforms continuing to host passengers. Latrobe, Pennsylvania, is a flag stop served by Amtrak's daily *Pennsylvania* (New York–Philadelphia–Pittsburgh) and passengers board the train from track-level platforms. However, the old railroad station building has been adapted into a popular railroad-themed restaurant. This view of Latrobe's former Pennsylvania Railroad station was made from the Amtrak platform in 2011. *Brian Solomon*

Opposite: Kansas City Southern built this asymmetrical Spanish Colonial Revival–style railroad station at DeQuncy, Louisiana, in 1923. At one time it housed dispatching offices as well as passenger facilities. Typical of segregation-era railroad stations in the South, this building featured separate waiting rooms for white and black passengers. A half-century after it built the station, KCS transferred ownership to the community that now operates it as a local railroad museum. While KCS continues to operate freight on the line, the route has been void of regularly scheduled passenger services for decades. *Tom Kline*

situations the railroad lines adjacent to stations were abandoned, relocated, or downgraded, in others the tracks found renewed activity, especially after deregulation in the 1980s spurred the growth of freight traffic on many American mainlines. Yet, even when railroads found new life, rarely did they need their old stations.

REPURPOSED STATIONS

All across North America, old railroad station buildings have been transformed for a great variety of applications. Since station buildings are often prominent, well located, and solidly build structures with close ties to the communities they serve, they are ideally suited for civic purposes. They have been converted into local chambers of commerce offices, tourist centers, police stations, and libraries. The old New Haven Station at Southbridge, Massachusetts, has had an ironic repurposing: it is now the local Department of Motor Vehicles, now that a passenger train hasn't served the town in more than seventy years.

Restaurants are one of the most common types of station transformations. The general layout of

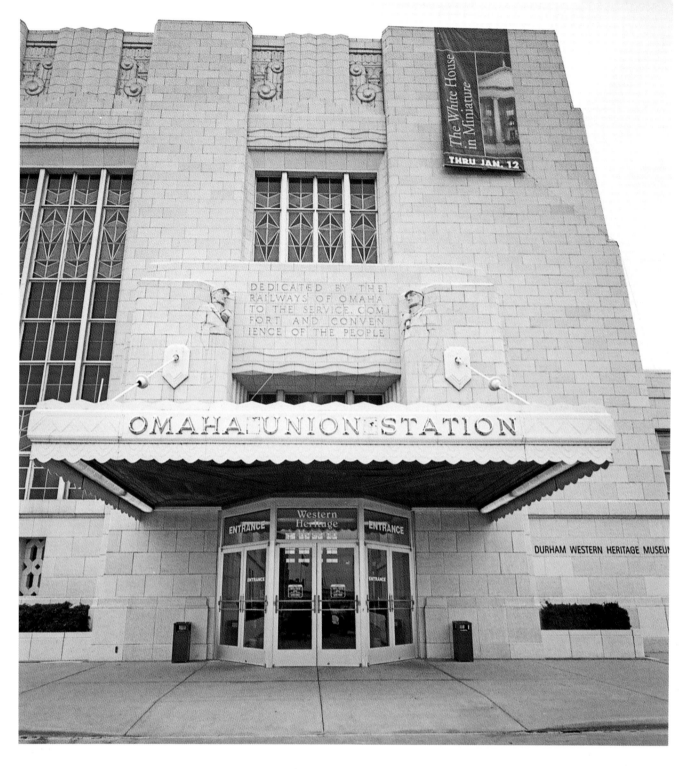

railroad stations, with large central waiting rooms and ample parking, makes these well suited for restaurant service. Plus, many stations would have housed restaurants in their heyday. The Steaming Tender in Palmer, Massachusetts; DiSalvo's Station at Latrobe, Pennsylvania; and *La Estacíon* in the old Chicago & North Western depot at Waukesha, Wisconsin, are among the numerous examples of trackside, railroad-themed eateries in old station buildings. In some situations, adjacent platforms are still active, which leads to the potential of

taking a train to the station for dinner—assuming that services are sufficiently convenient. Station buildings also make logical places for railroad museums and local historical societies, as well as private residences. In some cases, railroads have been willing to sell station buildings but insist they are moved away from the tracks, especially where main lines remain active.

Large stations, often the late-era architecturally significant wonders of the first decades of the twentieth century, are ideally suited as shopping plazas or museums.

These stations were designed for a large flow of people, with capacious waiting rooms and concourses, myriad supporting facilities, and ample space for multiple venues. Union stations at Richmond, Virginia; Cincinnati and Cleveland, Ohio; and St. Louis and Kansas City, Missouri, are grand examples of such stations transformed.

After old railroad station buildings have been repurposed as popular attractions, sometimes planners discover that these facilities with proximity to tracks and central urban locations make them ideal places to stop passenger trains.

RETURN TO GLORY

Some stations, built to show off a railroad's wealth in the golden years, represented the work of famous architects and may be among the finest buildings in town. As the railroad's passenger traffic declined, and the old

Opposite: Gilbert S. Underwood designed the Omaha (Nebraska) Union Station in the Art Deco style. This was completed in 1931 for Union Pacific, a railroad with operation headquarters in Omaha. While Union Pacific has grown to become one of the largest railroads in North America, it hasn't operated a regularly scheduled public passenger service since 1971 when it conveyed operations to Amtrak. UP donated the elegant historic structure to the city in the mid-1970s and it now houses the Durham Western History Museum. Amtrak's daily *California Zephyr* serves Omaha via BNSF's former Burlington route and uses a modern station building constructed in the 1980s a few blocks to the south of this structure. *Brian Solomon*

Below: An interior view of Underwood's Art Deco masterpiece, the Omaha Union Station. Consider the similarities between this station waiting room and Philadelphia's 30th Street Station pictured in Chapter 1. *Brian Solomon*

Top: It's often easy to identify an old railroad station by its characteristic architecture. This June 2005 photograph shows Morgan's Grocery at Penn Yan, New York, which occupies the old Pennsylvania Railroad Elmira Branch passenger station. In PRR days, this had been a heavy north-south route largely used to convey bituminous coal to Lake Ontario docks at Sodus Point. Local passenger service to Penn Yan survived through World War II but had ended by the mid-1950s. *Brian Solomon*

Bottom: Boston & Albany maintained separate passenger and freight stations at Gilbertville, Massachusetts, on its 50-mile-long Ware River Branch. Both structures survive, yet neither has been served by the railroad in decades. Today the tracks at the back of the buildings host freight trains operated by Massachusetts Central, which works the remaining 25 miles of line between Palmer, Gilbertville, and South Barre. The old passenger station serves as the Whistle Stop Café, conveniently located on Route 32 opposite the town's public library. *Brian Solomon*

109   *Aloe Plaza, Showing Fountain, Union Station and Post Office, St. Louis, Mo.*

1B-H35

Top: Salt Lake City was an important destination on the Union Pacific and warranted construction of an impressive station. Daniel J. Patterson designed this building in the French Renaissance Revival style, featuring a prominent steeply pitched slate mansard roof. Union Pacific occupied the building until the mid-1980s, then donated it to the State of Utah. It has since been carefully restored and now serves as the multi-function plaza called *Grand Entrance to the Gateway*, which hosts entertainment, retail shops, and restaurants. *Brian Solomon*

Bottom: St. Louis was one of the principal east-west gateway cities. Its large Union Station was operated by Terminal Railroad Association of St. Louis and hosted trains of twenty-two railroad companies. *Period postcard, Solomon collection*

downtown with its narrow streets and a dearth of public parking became unfashionable, the station as well as the area around it slowly decayed. New development occurred along new highways out along "the strip." For decades, the old station was neglected, its roof sprouting small bushes and its windows boarded up. Yet the building survived, serving as a skeletal reminder of the era when Americans shopped downtown and took the train.

But finally, after many years, downtown again becomes popular. Planners eyeing means for urban renewal focused on the old railroad station. Architects were consulted, building contractors lined up, and the old building put back together and made to look new again. Sometimes the trains come back, other times the building thrives repurposed. Today, all across the country, there are dozens of examples of beautifully restored stations.

Yet, many other stations still await their return to glory. Like gazing upon the phoenix, theirs is certain joy when an old station is restored. The old nexus of transportation is again useful. This is especially true when the old building was the work of a great architect.

Above: Today, the classic Kansas City terminal building is owned by a nonprofit organization called Union Station Kansas City, Inc., which aims for continued preservation of the building along with its history. This view of the front of the station was made in September 2000. Today the station building is home to a variety of attractions including a planetarium, cinemas, and museums. *Tom Kline*

Right: The passenger concourse and waiting rooms at Kansas City Union Station were designed to awe travelers. In 1916, author John A. Droege pointed out in *Passenger Terminals and Trains* that Kansas City was unusual among larger terminals because it catered almost entirely to long-distance passengers and was virtually without commuter traffic. *Tom Kline*

Opposite top: Historically, Southern Pacific's Golden State route met the Rock Island Lines at Santa Rosa, New Mexico. However, in practice, SP and Rock interchanged trains many miles to the east at Tucumcari, where in the mid-1920s Southern Pacific built this impressive Spanish Mission-style station. Once a division point for famous named trains such as the *Golden State* and the *Imperial,* by the time of this 1994 photo, it was tired-looking vision of former glory. The station building has since been restored. Union Pacific now operates the *Golden State* route as part of its transcontinental freight network. *Brian Solomon*

Opposite bottom: The union station at Tacoma, Washington, was designed by Reed & Stem, well-known architects based in St. Paul, Minnesota, who in addition to working on stations for Northern Pacific contributed to the design of New York City's Grand Central Terminal. When it opened in 1911, Tacoma Union Station served trains operated by Great Northern, Northern Pacific, and Union Pacific. It was last used by Amtrak in the early 1980s and has since been adapted for use as a federal courthouse. *Tom Kline*

Above: Kansas City Union Station's importance as a railway terminal declined rapidly in the 1950s as railroads began trimming their passenger schedules. Although long-distance services continued with the coming of Amtrak in 1971, the station was only a shadow compared with former years. Amtrak vacated in the mid-1980s, and the station building was restored in the late 1990s. It now hosts museums, shops, and restaurants and, since Amtrak's return, a small station as well. *Tom Kline*

Below: The interior of Kansas City Union Station as it appeared in the early 1940s. The station's Beaux Arts design was the work of Jarvis Hunt, who is also known for his Joliet, Illinois, Union Station and Southern Pacific's 16th Street Station in Oakland, California. *Period postcard, Solomon collection*

HENRY HOBSON RICHARDSON'S NEW ENGLAND STATIONS

New England railroads enjoyed robust growth in the decades following the Civil War. Many of these lines were among the earliest in the United States to be surveyed and laid out, but postwar growth saw a rapid swell of traffic that accelerated the consolidation of smaller companies into regional systems, along with large-scale improvements to existing properties. Among the notable infrastructure investments were grade separations that coincided with replacement stations.

By the 1880s, many of the original wooden frame stations built during the formative years of railroading became both functionally and stylistically outmoded. Prosperous railroads justified new investments to both impress the public and to accommodate traffic growth.

Henry Hobson Richardson was among the most important architects of his generation. In the right place at the right time to benefit from the New England railroads' late-nineteenth-century prosperity, he helped define a new era of station design. There could be no better time, as the railroads in the region were approaching the zenith of their wealth and influence. In the book *H. H. Richardson: Complete Architectural Works* (1981), Jeffery Karl Ochsner described Richardson as

Kansas City Union Station was built by the Kansas City Terminal Railway for KCTRy's twelve owning railroads and functioned as a transfer point between Midwestern and Western lines. The building was designed by Jarvis Hunt and it opended in 1914. This contemporary view shows the terminal building after its 1990s restoration. *Tom Kline*

one "of the four giants of American architecture." Yet, Richardson's work is also rare to find still standing. Only a few of his stations remain, and these remain obscure.

Richardson's career spanned from 1866 to 1886; Ochsner credits him with more than 150 architectural plans (not all executed), many of which were railway stations or related structures. He is best known for his Romanesque style. His design of Boston's Trinity Church is perhaps his most famous work. Many of his commissions were ecclesial buildings or domestic residences. Richardson's railroad works were largely the result of influential friendships, including with two of Boston & Albany's (B&A) directors.

James A. Rumhill was a former classmate and longtime friend of Richardson's, who in 1880 became a B&A vice president and a year later was appointed to the board of directors. Rumhill also served in an influential capacity with New London & Northern (later a component of the Central Vermont), and both lines awarded Richardson with significant commissions.

In addition, Richardson's neighbor was Charles S. Sargent, another up-and-coming B&A director.

In the 1880s, B&A began a massive upgrading of its suburban services west of Boston that resulted in planning for many new station buildings on both its mainline and the parallel Highland Branch through Newton, Massachusetts. B&A took an unusual approach toward commuter services and developed its Highland branch as part of a circular route from its Kneeland Street terminal in Boston. This double-track branch was assembled from trackage acquired from other railroads plus new construction to form a "circuit" that tied into the mainline at two locations, the western-most being at Riverside, west of Newton. This gave the railroad great operational flexibility while allowing it to better serve some of Boston's most affluent suburbs.

Richardson's first commission with the B&A was in 1881 for a new suburban station at Auburndale, 10.3 miles west of Boston. This set several precedents for his later works. In conjunction with this project, Richardson worked with landscape architect Frederick Law Olmsted to create surrounding gardens and park space. Olmsted is best known for his work on Central Park in Manhattan, and Richardson routinely collaborated with him on major projects. The station was constructed from granite and trimmed with brownstone. This was a straightforward

Above: Among the surviving H. H. Richardson stations in the Boston area is this building at Wellesley Hills, Massachusetts, along the former Boston & Albany main line, located 13.5 miles from Boston's South Station. Although MBTA commuter trains still serve the platforms, the old station building has been adapted for other businesses including a dry cleaner. Significantly, it is one of the few Richardson stations that retains elements of its original nineteenth-century Olmsted landscaping. *Brian Solomon*

Opposite top: In the 1880s, when Boston & Albany commissioned Henry Hobson Richardson, one of America's most distinguished architects, to design stations along its lines, it was a very prosperous railroad with robust passenger traffic. The Union Station at Palmer, Massachusetts, was the second building to be completed by Richardson and entered service in 1884. B&A was leased by New York Central in 1900. The station saw its last regular passenger train in the 1960s. By the time of this nocturnal photograph in May 1985, the old station was a shadow of its former glory. *Brian Solomon*

Opposite bottom: A Conrail track crew cleans snow from the switches on the former Boston & Albany mainline at Framingham, Massachusetts, on November 26, 1985. The former B&A South Framingham station (as the location was originally known) is one of a handful of surviving station buildings designed by H. H. Richardson. Completed in 1885, it was a characteristic example of the Romanesque style. Alterations from the original plan include the exterior spiral staircases and related modifications to the roof. It is among the Richardson stations adapted for use as a restaurant. *Brian Solomon*

suburban station, yet featured a small ticket office and baggage room, with individual waiting rooms for men and women. Platforms were covered by long roof extensions that maintained the stylistic continuity of the structure.

Over the next five years, nine B&A stations were built to Richardson's plans, most of which also benefited from Olmsted's landscaping. The majority of Richardson's B&A stations were built in Boston suburban territory, including three small halts along the Highland Branch at Eliot, Waban, and Woodland.

Interestingly, the second B&A station to be completed was the new Palmer, Massachusetts, Union Station, neatly situated between mainlines of both B&A and New London Northern. This was constructed between 1883 and 1885 to replace an older building dating to the 1830s, built by the Western Railroad (of Massachusetts), a B&A predecessor that had been located on the north side of the B&A tracks facing Palmer's "Depot Village." Construction was executed by W. N. Flynt & Company, a local firm that also built a similarly styled structure opposite the B&A tracks on the approximate location of the old station (which was sold and moved to another location for non-railroad use).

Palmer's station was faced with locally quarried Monson granite (the quarry was located a few miles south of Palmer and accessed via a short branch off the New London & Northern) and trimmed with Longmeadow brownstone from the nearby town of the same name. Owing to the constraints on its placement between active railway lines, the station has an unusual shape and layout. It has a nearly triangular floor plan, with its longest side facing the New London & Northern line, with the point of the station truncated near the "Palmer diamonds" where the two railroads crossed at grade. The station was reached by a driveway on the southeastern side, and in its original configuration it benefited from an elegant Olmstead park located between B&A and NL&N lines. The park featured a semicircular stone grotto. Near the diamonds, a pedestrian "subway" gave passengers easy access to downtown Palmer by directing them to a street below, which obviated the need to cross tracks at grade.

The former Boston & Albany Highland Branch station at Newton Centre, Massachusetts, was designed by Shepley, Rutan & Coolidge and constructed in 1891. It exhibits many classic Richardsonian features, including solid brownstone construction, extended platform canopies that are integral with the main structure, eyelid dormer windows, and a slate roof. It was photographed with an inbound MBTA Green Line Boeing-Vertol light rail vehicle. The old B&A branch was converted to light-rail rapid transit in the late 1950s. In 2015, the station building was occupied by the Deluxe Station Diner, which also operates a similar restaurant in the old B&A Framingham Station. *Brian Solomon*

Above: Boston & Albany's Union Station at Chatham, New York, hasn't served as a railroad station in more than four decades. The building was restored in the 1990s, including a new slate roof, and is now home to a branch of the National Union Bank of Kinderhook. The adjacent railroad is now operated by CSX, which operates 16–20 freights daily plus Amtrak's *Lake Shore Limited*, which passes Chatham without stopping. *Brian Solomon*

Right: Architect Henry Hobson Richardson died in 1886, and his commission to design Boston & Albany Railroad stations went to Boston architects Shepley, Rutan & Coolidge who designed twenty-three stations for the B&A in Richardson's Romanesque style. The union station at Chatham, New York, was completed in 1887 and served B&A and its corporate successors into the early 1970s. It was derelict at the time of this May 1988 photograph. *Brian Solomon*

LEGACY OF RICHARDSONIAN INFLUENCE

Richardson Romanesque is among the most recognizable American styles and one especially well-suited to railroad station design. Sadly, H. H. Richardson died in 1886 at age forty-eight, at the peak of his career. His commissions for Boston & Albany and other railroad stations were carried out by his successors, Shepley, Rutan & Coolidge. Charles A. Coolidge was among Richardson's protégés who had studied architecture under him. Ochsner points out that "the transition from projects by Richardson to those of . . . Shepley, Rutan, and Coolidge, is a subtle one."

These architects were well versed in the style and motifs of their master, and their Richardsonian interpretations could easily be passed off as those of Richardson himself. This is especially true in regard to the B&A stations. They completed twenty-three stations for the B&A between 1887 and 1894. While Shepley, Rutan & Coolidge adhered to the pattern established by Richardson,

incorporating his classic trademark features—including weighty solid designs with prominent use of architectural features such as arches and eyelid dormer windows—they didn't push this style to the same extremes as Richardson had. Shepley, Rutan & Coolidge went on to accept other commissions, including the station head house for Boston's South Station (featured in Chapter 1).

Richardson's railroad influence went well beyond those few stations that he personally designed and those designed by his immediate successors. B&A adopted

his style, as did other railroads in the region. In addition to Shepley, Rutan & Coolidge, some of B&A's Richardsonian structures have been attributed to the railroad's engineering department. Richardson's one-time assistants, Charles McKim and Stanford White, went on to become some of the most prominent railway station architects of American railroad's golden age. McKim, Mead & White were responsible for New York's magnificent Pennsylvania Station (see Chapter 3), among other structures.

Above and opposite: The story of Palmer Union Station is a happy one. In the mid-2000s, the building's interior was largely restored to its original appearance and today serves as the popular Steaming Tender Restaurant. This railroad-themed eatery is a great place for a meal and to watch trains. CSX's former B&A mainline runs on the north side of the station, while New England Central's former Central Vermont line is on the south side. The two railroads cross immediately west of the building. *Brian Solomon*

LEASE, DECLINE, AND TRANSFORMATION

In 1900, the Vanderbilt-controlled New York Central & Hudson River Railroad leased the Boston & Albany Railroad. The B&A's lines remained part of the New York Central Railroad, despite retaining a degree of autonomy through the end of the steam era. B&A's tracks swelled with passenger and freight traffic in the early twentieth century, but after World War I entered a long period of slow decline. As elsewhere in North America, the railroad enjoyed a traffic resurgence during World War II and then faced precipitous declines, especially in its long-distance passenger business in the postwar era. The New York Central Railroad made one last effort to improve

local and suburban passenger business in the early 1950s when it placed modern Budd Rail Diesel Cars in service on the B&A. These were advertised as "Bee Liners," and for several years their flashy stainless-steel appearance made for a stunning contrast to B&A's Richardsonian brownstone stations.

Construction of the Massachusetts Turnpike began in the 1950s and doomed B&A local services. This multi-lane, grade-separated toll road ran parallel to B&A, and once it was integrated with the national Interstate Highway System as I-90, it virtually eliminated any remaining local passenger traffic outside the Boston suburbs.

Two parallel changes had an especially devastating effect on B&A infrastructure and architecture. After

World War II, Boston's Metropolitan Transit Authority (MTA)—predecessor to the Massachusetts Bay Transportation Authority created in the mid-1960s—gradually pared back the city's electric streetcar system, replacing old trolley routes with buses and trolley buses. Despite this trend toward highway-based transport and a rapidly growing dependence on automobiles, in 1957 MTA opted to acquire the B&A Highland Branch from New York Central and convert this into a modern trolley-operated transit line. This opened for service with PCC cars in July 1959 as the Riverside Line. Unfortunately for building architecture, the trolley operations don't require station facilities. Several classic stations were demolished during the transition to trolley operations, including Richardson-designed buildings in the Boston suburban towns of Eliot and Waban. Other station buildings survived, notably Shepley, Rutan & Coolidge stations in the Massachusetts towns of Newton Centre and Newton Highland. Except, perhaps for their platform canopies, these historic buildings have been repurposed for non-railway uses.

The other significant change was the extension of the Massachusetts Turnpike east from Newton into downtown Boston, parallel to the B&A mainline. To make room for the toll road, two of the four tracks were lifted and the right of way widened. In the process, most of the remaining stations on this portion of the line were demolished, including Richardson's first B&A project at Auburndale. All evidence of these precedent-setting structures, once deemed as some of the most beautiful railway architecture in the United States, were destroyed to make way for the new mode of transport.

Elsewhere along the B&A route some old stations survived, although most were sold off to third parties for new uses. One of the finest remaining Richardson B&A stations outside the Boston suburban area is the old Palmer Union Station. This hosted its last regular passenger services in the mid-1960s, and was later transferred to private ownership. During the Conrail era, the truncated vestiges of Richardson's canopies on its B&A side were removed, which unfortunately altered the

NJ Transit's Hoboken Terminal is used by suburban trains on both former Lackawanna and Erie Railroad routes. It is among the stations designed by Kenneth W. Murchison and opened in 1907 to replace earlier terminal facilities destroyed in a spectacular fire. *Brian Solomon*

intended appearance of the building and destroyed the architect's carefully balanced design.

After years of slow decline, when it variously hosted a lunch counter and pool hall and an antique shop, it was beautifully restored for use as the *Steaming Tender* railroad-themed restaurant. Inside the station, Richardson's late-Victorian splendor makes for a popular venue to socialize over a meal and watch passing trains. Outside, the station is still undergoing restoration, as is the adjacent old Olmsted park.

RICHARDSON BEYOND THE B&A

In addition to his work solely for B&A, Richardson also designed stations for New London & Northern Railroad owing to the influence of his friend Rumhill. New London, Connecticut, Union Station was a large building designed to serve passengers of both NL&N and New Haven Railroads, as well as NL&N divisional offices. This impressive building survives as Amtrak's New London station for the North East Corridor route. Ironically, the NL&N line, later a core part of Central Vermont's Palmer Subdivision, discontinued regular passenger service in the 1940s, although the route survives for freight.

Other Richardson stations included buildings for other New England lines, among them an impressive station along the Connecticut River Railroad (later part of the Boston & Maine system) at Holyoke, Massachusetts. This is one of a handful of surviving Richardson railroad stations, but as of this writing (2015) remained in poor condition, its overall state a reflection of Holyoke's long industrial decline. Interestingly, Holyoke was recently put back on the passenger map as Amtrak's *Vermonter* was rerouted via the Connecticut River line between Springfield and Greenfield. Despite the revitalization of the route and local interest in the old Richardson building, a new station was built nearby with facilities deemed to be better suited for today's passenger requirements, notably parking and handicapped access, and providing significantly better access to downtown Holyoke.

KENNETH M. MURCHISON MASTERPIECES

William H. Truesdale assumed control of the anthracite coal-hauling Delaware, Lackawanna & Western Railroad (DL&W) in 1899, and during the early twentieth century, he transformed DL&W into a modern railroad with state-of-the-art infrastructure. His skillful management and massive capital improvements were designed to lower the railroad's costs and make it more competitive. Among Truesdale's projects were expensive line relocations and massive terminal improvements. During this Lackawanna renaissance, Kenneth M. Murchison was hired to design the railroad's finest passenger facilities.

Murchison was a respected New York architect who earned several important commissions for railroad stations in the early twentieth century. He had studied in Paris and made prominent use of the Beaux Arts style in his railway architecture. Among his significant early projects was DL&W's new Hoboken Terminal on the west shore of the Hudson River across from New York City. Replacing an earlier facility that had succumbed to fire, this elaborate station complex made prominent

This view of Hoboken's main waiting room was exposed during the midday lull on January 15, 2015. Architect Kenneth W. Murchison was a student of the École des Beaux-Arts in Paris and was inspired by the French Baroque for his styling of the station. Hoboken Terminal underwent an extensive restoration between 2004 and 2011 that included work on its ferry slips. *Brian Solomon*

use of copper sheathing believed to be leftover from the construction of the *Statue of Liberty* in nearby Upper New York Harbor.

Murchison followed up his success with Hoboken with an impressive five-story station for the DL&W at Scranton, Pennsylvania, constructed in 1908. Scranton was Lackawanna's mecca; this coal-producing city was at the very heart of Lackawanna's empire. Lackawanna had begun here in 1849 as a broad gauge feeder to the Erie Railroad and later developed into one of the Erie's primary competitors. In its early years, its primary line extended north from Scranton to a connection with Erie at Great Bend, New York, east of Binghamton.

Anthracite was key to DL&W's growth; this was reflected in its route structure and later in advertising motifs for its passenger services. By the second half of the

After the end of regular passenger services, the former Delaware, Lackawanna & Western main passenger station at Scranton was abandoned. Then during the 1980s it was redeveloped as a hotel and now serves as the Radisson Lackawanna Station Hotel. This World War I-era nocturnal painting shows the station in its glory years as one of the most important passenger stations on the Lackawanna system. *Period postcard, Solomon collection*

nineteenth century, DL&W had expanded eastward across the Poconos to the Delaware River, eventually reaching Hoboken, New Jersey, while later stretching west across New York State to Buffalo, New York. It extended secondary lines to Utica, New York, and to the important coal port on Lake Ontario at Oswego, New York.

In those days, moving anthracite was a lucrative business, as this clean-burning coal was the choice fuel for home heating. The railroad reaped healthy profit from its anthracite business, and its operations were focused at Scranton, where it built sprawling yards and shops. In the early twentieth century, Lackawanna launched a legendary advertising campaign featuring the pure, demure (and totally fictional) passenger, "Phoebe Snow," who was represented in magazines and newspapers along with catchy ditties, aimed at simultaneously promoting Lackawanna's premier New York to Buffalo *Lackawanna*

Limited while advocating the virtues of Pennsylvania anthracite. The most famous of Lackawanna's rhymes:

> *Says Phoebe Snow*
> *About to go*
> *Upon a trip*
> *To Buffalo*
> *My gown stays white*
> *From morn till night*
> *Upon the Road of Anthracite.*

The importance of Scranton to Lackawanna, and to the competition from a host of other railroads here, mandated magnificence on the part of DL&W's new Scranton Station. Murchison was the right man for the job. Working in French-Renaissance style characteristic of the Beaux Arts movement, Murchison imparted Continental elegance on this Pennsylvania coal capital. He used massive colonnades on both the street and track sides of the station and maintained classic symmetry. At the center of the roofline, an enormous clock was flanked by stone eagles. The building was faced with Indiana limestone. An unusually deep hanging canopy encircled the structure to protect passengers when

Above: Kenneth M. Murchison's great station designs include the Jacksonville Union Terminal at Jacksonville, Florida. Completed in 1919, this served four major railroads. In the 1980s, following years of neglect, it was transformed as part of the new Prime F. Osborn III convention center, named for a former CSX chairman. (CSX, one of the largest freight railroads in the eastern United States, is headquartered in Jacksonville.) *Period postcard, Solomon collection*

Right: Hoboken Terminal is clad in copper plate. For many years this was a dingy relic of former times, but this amazing terminal has undergone several extensive restorations in recent years. It is now a tribute of the Lackawanna Railroad of which only vestiges survive. *Brian Solomon*

arriving and boarding trains, while smokeless sheds, originally designed by DL&W chief engineer Lincoln Bush for Hoboken, were installed trackside. In the 1920s an additional story was added.

After World War I, the demand for anthracite waned and both Lackawanna and Scranton suffered. Although the railroad continued to carry robust freight and passenger traffic into the late 1940s, the continued shift away from anthracite as a home heating fuel and a general decline of heavy industry along DL&W's lines through the 1950s weighed heavily on the line's future. In 1949, on the fiftieth anniversary of the inauguration of the original *Lackawanna Limited*, DL&W introduced its plush new streamliner officially called *The Phoebe Snow*.

By the mid-1950s, Lackawanna became financially desperate and implemented some cost-saving consolidations with Erie that included Erie's Hoboken-destined trains moving to DL&W's terminal. Then in 1960 the two longtime competitors merged to form Erie Lackawanna, resulting in further consolidations. DL&W's route east from Binghamton via Scranton was the preferred passenger line. However, rising passenger deficits in the 1960s resulted in Erie Lackawanna discontinuing all long-distance services prior to Amtrak. Historically, DL&W's Hoboken Terminal served both long-distance and commuter trains. DL&W's Hoboken Terminal remained an important commuter rail station, but it decayed and by the mid-1980s was a functioning ruin. It was restored in the 1990s with further work in recent years.

Meanwhile, by the 1970s, DL&W's Scranton Station was abandoned. Erie Lackawanna was among eastern railroads bailed out by the creation of Conrail in 1976. However, Conrail planners deemphasized the Erie Lackawanna routes, a move that resulted in diversion of most through traffic away from Scranton. Visitors to the city in the early 1980s were greeted by depressing scenes of dilapidation and industrial decay. Murchison's masterpiece sat in tatters, its windows broken and its upper floors filled with pigeons.

It was during this nadir that many eastern railroad stations were unceremoniously demolished. Happily, DL&W's Scranton Station had another fate. In the mid-1980s, the property was redeveloped as a hotel, today operated as Radisson Lackawanna Station Hotel. The nearby former DL&W shops have become the home of the Steamtown collection of locomotives and historic railway equipment. Originally a private foundation based in Vermont, the collection was relocated to Scranton in part because of local political support. In 1986 the Steamtown National Historic Site was created, and since that time the National Park Service has assumed management and operation of the equipment collection with the site of the Scranton shops preserved and adapted as a railroad museum.

BALTIMORE

Another of Murchison's attractive stations is Baltimore's Pennsylvania Station (originally Baltimore Union Station) that opened on September 15, 1911. Like his Scranton

Station, this embodies a Beaux Arts neoclassical design, replacing an older station at the same location that served PRR predecessor Northern Central. Murchison's Baltimore Station is four stories tall, the two upper floors serving as offices, with a two-story main waiting room. It is constructed from pink Milford granite from Massachusetts, with an interior faced with Pentelic and Sicilian marble. While principal passenger areas—waiting rooms and ticket counters—are at street level, tracks are located below. Murchison worked with Lincoln Bush on this project, and Baltimore features Bush-style train sheds. Like other American stations, it suffered from

the decline of passenger services. It was restored in the mid-1980s and today serves both Amtrak long-distance trains (including its high-speed *Acela Express*) and MARC's regional suburban trains.

RICHMOND (VA) UNION STATION

John Russell Pope (1874–1937) was among America's foremost early-twentieth-century architects. Born in New York City to an artistic family, he studied architecture under William R. Ware at Columbia University and furthered his architectural education at the École des Beaux-Arts in Paris, the school that set the

Richmond, Virginia's Broad Street Station, otherwise known as Union Station, was designed by John Russell Pope and constructed for the Richmond Terminal Railway between 1917 and 1919. Originally it served passenger trains for Richmond, Fredericksburg & Potomac and Atlantic Coast Line. Amtrak stopped using the neoclassical station in 1975 in favor of its modern suburban facility at Staples Mills Road. Broad Street Station was considered for demolition but instead was transformed into The Science Museum of Virginia. *Brian Solomon*

tone for many great railway station designs. He worked as an assistant to Charles F. McKim of McKim, Meade & White. In 1912, Pope married into a wealthy social family that provided access to many influential clients.

Pope applied neoclassical design in the Beaux Arts tradition. He is best known for prominent buildings in Washington, DC, including the National Archives and Jefferson Memorial. Richmond Union Station in Virginia was his only railway station commission; its classical symmetry and towering dome above the floor lend obvious similarity to his design for the Jefferson Memorial.

Richmond Union Station, located at Broad Street, was built for the Richmond Terminal Railway between 1917 and 1919. It was constructed to serve passenger trains operated by Richmond, Fredericksburg & Potomac and Atlantic Coast Line. Richmond, Virginia, is famous for its prominent role during the Civil War, and this new terminal was built on the site of military encampments, later fairgrounds, on the western fringe of the city.

Like many late-era urban stations, the station building was built above track level. Carroll Meeks compares it to designs of Kansas City and Baltimore Union Stations that were built to a similar pattern a few years earlier, where a bridge waiting room formed an enclosed gallery "connected by stairs with the several platforms immediately below, so the passenger waiting there has the comfort of being Johnny-on-the-spot."

In the early 1970s, after Amtrak assumed operation of intercity passenger services, it phased out Richmond's Union Station in favor of an entirely new suburban facility at Staples Mills Road that better suited its operational requirements. Pope's neoclassic gem saw its last regularly scheduled passenger train in November 1975. The property was acquired by the Commonwealth of Virginia, which initially planned to demolish the station building to make room for a modern office complex. Instead, the station was redeveloped as The Science Museum of Virginia. Although this was initially a temporary arrangement, it has been made permanent and in recent years the station building has benefited from a multimillion-dollar renovation. Today, it hosts a variety of exhibits including an IMAX Theater and is open to the public daily.

Opposite: Author Carroll Meeks described Cincinnati Union Station's great arch as "the unchallenged giant of station portals."
Brian Solomon

FELLHEIMER AND WAGNER: A TALE OF THREE TERMINALS

After the mid-1920s, the golden age of railroads was over, and the age of the automobile was underway. The years of exponential growth had ended and railroad passenger services entered their long decline as the business eroded. Despite that, some lines remained optimistic about the future of the passenger train, so in the late 1920s and early 1930s a few new major terminals were built.

Three of the most interesting late-era big stations were designed by architects Fellheimer and Wagner at Boston, Massachusetts; Buffalo, New York; and Cincinnati, Ohio. These massive modern stations embodied Art Deco styling with unusual European influences, including Saarinen's groundbreaking Helsinki station discussed in the next chapter. (Fellheimer worked as a junior architect on the Beaux Arts Grand Central in New York and integrated some of its advanced ideas on circulation and natural lighting into his later, mostly Art Deco, works.) Construction of Boston's and Buffalo's new stations began in 1927. Boston's North Station was built combining a big city railway terminal (along with all of the usual facilities, including railroad offices) with a major sports stadium featuring thousands of seats.

Ironically while Boston's terminal was first to open (1928) and remained the busiest—enjoying a sustained suburban traffic through the lean years between 1960 and the 1980s—it was the least interesting architecturally, and is the only one of the three that no longer stands. North Station was a victim of its prime location. While the North Station itself remains one of two primary Boston terminals, Fellheimer and Wagner's station building was demolished in the 1990s to make way for a modern station and improved stadium above it.

Of the two surviving Fellheimer and Wagner terminals, both remain as Art Deco icons and serve as symbols of the false optimism that faced railroads in the late-1920s. Their fates have followed different paths: Although now the subject of an ambitious preservation effort, for decades Buffalo Terminal has been a colossal urban ruin and ominous specter on the Buffalo skyline seeming to symbolize the decay of a once great urban center and the end of the passenger era. By contrast, Cincinnati Union Station survived threats of obliteration and was successfully adapted into a museum and conference center that retains its aura of Art Deco elegance.

BUFFALO CENTRAL TERMINAL

Buffalo, New York's Queen City, was historically the second-most important metropolis in the Empire State. In the nineteenth and early twentieth centuries, Buffalo enjoyed rapid urban growth stemming from its strategic location at the east end of Lake Erie. It developed as an important railroad gateway, where Eastern lines met those from the Midwest and Canada. Of the eight major railroads serving Buffalo, New York Central System had by far the most important presence and was the only line with significant through traffic. Buffalo was the traditional meeting point of the New York Central & Hudson River Railroad with its western sisters, Lake Shore & Michigan Southern and Michigan Central lines, with which it formed through routes to Chicago. Buffalo was also approximately halfway between New York and Chicago, giving it added significance on this long-distance passenger run.

The strategic importance of Buffalo to New York Central warranted an impressive passenger terminal, yet the old station near downtown was too hemmed in by urban growth to permit the sort of modern facility deemed necessary. As a result, New York Central opted to locate its new terminal two miles west of its existing

Above: New York Central was America's second-busiest passenger carrier. It's famed "Great Steel Fleet" connected New York City with Chicago and numerous other cities across New York State and the Midwest. On May 26, 1961, a pair of New York Central Electro-Motive E-units (an E7A and E8A) lead a westward train at Buffalo on a gray day, typical of spring weather along the Great Lakes. Although the railroad's passenger service was in decline, Buffalo Central Terminal still hosted dozens of daily passenger trains. *Richard Jay Solomon*

Opposite: Canadian Pacific affiliate Toronto, Hamilton & Buffalo was among the railroads to join New York Central at Buffalo Central Terminal. While in later years its services were provided by a Budd RDC, this May 26, 1961, photograph shows a conventional train complete with a baggage car jointly operated by TH&B, Canadian Pacific, and New York Central. Looming above the train in the distance is the terminal's iconic Art Deco sixteen-story office tower. An entrance to the ramp leading to the concourse can be seen at far left. *Richard Jay Solomon*

The Electro-Motive E-unit in the classic postwar "Lightening Stripe" livery typified New York Central's long distance passenger locomotive in the diesel era. Central's E8A 4061 leads a westward train at Buffalo. *Richard Jay Solomon*

station. While this permitted ample space for a massive and impressive station, it posed problems in later years as the terminal was not conveniently situated for passengers. By traditional standards, it was not close enough to downtown, but in later years it wasn't sufficiently far away from downtown to serve the growing Buffalo suburbs

Plans and preparations for the new Buffalo Terminal complex began in 1926, and construction commenced in 1927. The terminal arrangement consisted of a large rectangular terminal building built above track level with an overhead concourse and ramps used to reach seven lengthy platforms. As noted, Fellheimer's overall plan

In September 2000, with many of its windows broken and its halls and rooms long empty, Buffalo Central Terminal stood as a dismal colossal urban ruin. Decades had passed since it was last used by passengers. Yet the thunder from CSX freight trains on the former New York Central mainline immediately south of the station served as a reminder of the continued importance of the American railroad as a freight network. *Brian Solomon*

was strongly influenced by Eliel Saarinen's Art Nouveau Helsinki Main Station (see Chapter 5) but constructed on a superhuman scale. The European Art Nouveau movement of the late nineteenth century embraced curvilinear natural forms that anticipated the streamlined minimalism characterized by the Art Deco styles that became popular in the late 1920s. Saarinen's use of a gigantic central arch and tower were interpreted by Fellheimer and Wagner to resemble an enormous radio set of the period. The sixteen-story office tower took the place of Saarinen's more modest clock tower and was visible from a great distance on the flat terrain of western New York State, rising 271 feet above ground and lit from below in the evening, making it an enormous beacon.

Buffalo Central Terminal never lived up to its intended role. Built for an anticipated flow of 10,000 daily passengers, it opened several months after the great Wall Street crash of October 1929, which had sent the American economy and the New York Central's traffic into a tailspin. Complicating matters, some of Buffalo's other railroads refused to use the station, opting instead to continue to serve their existing facilities. Toronto, Hamilton & Buffalo was among the carriers to join New York Central, but its passenger business was comparatively modest. And as previously mentioned, the station's remote location proved problematic, despite efforts to provide access for automobiles and public transport.

Yet for nearly a half-century, the Buffalo Central served passengers. Toward the end of its active years, it seemed like a ghastly hallmark of the decline of the American passenger train. The handful of surviving trains continuing to serve Buffalo represented only a fraction of those it intended to cater to, while the station's immense size greatly outweighed necessary funds to maintain it. Finally in 1979, Amtrak evacuated to a modest modern facility along the former New York Central mainline in suburban Depew, while its half-dozen Empire Service trains (New York City to Buffalo/Niagara Falls) continued to serve an even more modest stop at Exchange Street near downtown. By that time, the last vestige of the New York Central's once robust New York–Chicago service was Amtrak's once-per-day *Lake Shore Limited*.

The end of regular service left Buffalo Terminal an enormous largely vacant reminder of another era, or perhaps, an era that never was. Yet, this once awe-inspiring terminal has survived as an urban ruin, and despite the ravages of harsh western New York weather, an effort is underway to preserve and restore this amazing building. As of 2015, a nonprofit organization called the Central Terminal Restoration Corporation was actively raising funds and offering tours to preserve this national landmark. For more information, see www.buffalocentralterminal.org.

CINCINNATI (OH) UNION TERMINAL

Cincinnati Union Terminal has been deemed by many authors as America's finest example of railway architecture and among the last great American railway stations. It was planned during the 1920s, when optimism had few bounds and the future was bright. It shares many parallels with the Buffalo Terminal and required extensive urban reorganization and planning to make way for its construction, which began in August 1929 on the eve of the Great Depression. Despite the terrible blow to the economy, the terminal was completed ahead of schedule and was formally opened on March 31, 1933.

It was a rare bright spot in dark times for American railroading. The size and scope of the station speaks volumes about the importance of railroad passenger

transport to Cincinnati at the time of its construction. The whole of the facility, including tracks, platforms, and supporting yards required an estimated 287 acres. It was built to accommodate 216 daily trains carrying up to 17,000 passengers. Like many late-era railway projects, its relevance was overshadowed by other modes and it never really fulfilled the vision of its planners.

Despite disappointing utilization, Cincinnati Union Station remains as Fellheimer & Wagner's magnum opus. Its architecture must be viewed as means to an end, not merely a work of static art. This station's beauty was meant to be judged by its success as a transportation hub, not just as a massive modern structure designed to look impressive at a distance or from the bewildered eye of a tourist in transit.

Fellheimer and Wagner's Art Deco masterpiece at Cincinnati is all but idle on a cool, wet evening, October 25, 2002. The station's enormous main arch was inspired by Eliel Saarinen's Helsinki Main Station. *Brian Solomon*

Not everyone was impressed: Carroll Meeks, writing in the 1950s, was not awed by Cincinnati and judged its architects harshly, yet pointed out that "the conception was that of a half funnel laid out on the ground, the wide mouth gathering in the streams of travelers and the narrow end ejecting them onto platforms. Circulation was the fundamental consideration."

Key to their design was the immense concourse that extended across the array of tracks and platforms below. Like with their Buffalo Terminal, Fellheimer & Wagner

Above: Cincinnati Union's illustrative mosaic murals are the work of Winold Reiss. *Brian Solomon*

Below: Timekeeping is key to railroad operations and every great station has its clock, and Cincinnati Union Station's is unlikely to mistaken for any other. *Brian Solomon*

Opposite: Cincinnati Union Station's majestic dome spans 180 feet and rises to a height of 106 feet above the floor of the concourse. It's among the most impressive American stations ever built. *Brian Solomon*

used a system of ramps, instead of stairs, to deliver passengers to track level. On the city side of the station, passengers entered and exited the building at street level, where three sets of curving ramps were arranged as individual paths for automobiles and taxis, buses, and streetcars. The station's massive central arch was its most iconic feature. A dome towers above the concourse floor.

The dome and waiting areas were supremely decorated in the Art Deco style with characteristic motifs of the mid-1930s. It is this colorful cavernous space with texture provided by layers of plaster, painted in radiant colors and pastels that both offended Meeks' classical sentiments and awes modern visitors. Inside the concourse, colorful mosaic murals provided unique decoration. These were designed by Winold Reiss, who had been commissioned for the work.

It is difficult to fully appreciate Cincinnati Union Terminal's architecture today because in the 1970s the station's concourse extension over the platforms was

demolished to make way for expansion of the adjacent freight yards. Not only did the station cease to function as intended, but its essential design was amputated. Today, we can only appreciate the street-level portion of the building, while the majority of the track-level portion, once fundamental to the terminal's function, no longer exists.

This unfortunate disfigurement notwithstanding, the remainder of Cincinnati Union Terminal survived the destructive climate of the 1970s, and the city purchased the terminal building in 1975. In 1990 it was reopened as the Cincinnati Museum Center. Historically the terminal building served as a precursor to the modern-day shopping mall as well as a transport hub and offered passengers a great variety of amenities including a bookstore and newsstands, a cinema, clothing stores for adults, and a toy store, as well as cafés and a barber shop. Today these spaces are home to a variety of attractions, including the Cincinnati History Museum, Museum of Natural History and Science, Cincinnati History Library and Archive, and Duke Energy Children's Museum. Among the annual events held at Cincinnati Union Terminal is *Summerail*, where a wide selection of railway-themed audio-visual presentations is enjoyed by visitors, along with a popular railroadiana flea market.

Yet passenger transport plays only a relatively small role in Cincinnati Union Terminal today; Amtrak resumed service in 1992, and in 2015 its tri-weekly *Cardinal* (New York and Washington, DC, to Chicago) stops here, albeit in the early hours.

Dearborn Station served various Chicago railroads including the Erie, Grand Trunk Western, Santa Fe and Wabash. Although strategically located near the Loop, its facilities were cramped and outdated by the mid-twentieth century. The station closed to long distance traffic in 1971, when Amtrak consolidated its trains at the nearby Union Station. While the old shed was destroyed in 1976, the head house has been preserved, and today it is one of the few surviving Chicago terminal buildings. *Brian Solomon*

DEARBORN STATION CHICAGO

Chicago has long been America's railroad capital—where East meets West. Traditionally passengers traveling cross-country changed trains at Chicago, and many major railroads built mainlines toward this Midwestern hub. The myriad of overlapping and competing railroad networks serving Chicago had produced a complex maze of track, and no less than six major passenger terminals, which made life complicated for the interline traveler. Chicago Union Station served the Pennsylvania Railroad (and its affiliates), Burlington, Milwaukee Road, and the Alton Route; LaSalle Street Station was the domain of New York Central and Rock Island and also served erstwhile New York Central affiliate Nickel Plate Road; Chicago Grand Central (not to be mistaken with the New York City

Chicago's Dearborn Station head house faced the street at ground level. It was designed by Cyrus L.W. Eidlizt, a Swiss-born architect. Operated by Chicago & Western Indiana, this classic terminal station opened in 1885. It was altered following a fire in 1924 that destroyed its original steeply pitched roof and part of the adjacent clock tower. *Brian Solomon*

terminal) was home to minor passenger players, Baltimore & Ohio, Pere Marquette (part of the Chesapeake & Ohio system after World War II), Chicago Great Western, and Soo Line; and Illinois Central and Chicago & North Western had their own terminals, respectively known as Central Station and Chicago & North Western Station.

Chicago's sixth terminal, Dearborn, was built largely to serve the city's latecomers—railroads that didn't have their own terminal facilities and had to rely upon Chicago

Light snow covers the tracks on a frosty February evening at Denver Union Station. The *Rio Grande Ski Train* is being prepared for its journey over the Front Range to Winter Park the following morning. Since this 1997 view, Denver Union has been transformed into a multimodal transit center with new canopies augmenting traditional architecture. *Brian Solomon*

and Western Indiana for access and downtown terminal space. The station served long-distance trains from an eclectic mix of Eastern, Midwestern, and Western lines: Chicago & Eastern Illinois; Erie Railroad; Grand Trunk Western; Monon; Wabash; and Atchison, Topeka & Santa Fe. It also accommodated C&WI's own Chicago-area commuter trains.

stub-end terminals. It featured ticket offices, waiting rooms, and baggage areas in its classic head house located at ground level facing its namesake Chicago street. It was designed by Swiss-born architect Cyrus L. W. Eidlizt (1853–1921). Beyond the building was a large train shed spanning an open concourse and ten active tracks and platforms. The shed was an unusual wrought-iron design, relatively low and virtually concealed from a street-level view by the head-house architecture.

As with many late-nineteenth century terminals, Dearborn's original design was rapidly outmoded by rapid traffic growth. It received several expansions, including enclosure of the concourse in the 1920s. Unanticipated events resulted in more drastic changes. In 1924, a fire swept through the facility, destroying Eidlizt's steeply pitched roof and resulted in alteration and truncation of the twelve-story Romanesque fantasy-like clock tower—a structure uniquely styled among Midwestern structures and an icon of Chicago railroading.

There were several plans to replace Dearborn and other substandard terminals with more modern twentieth-century facilities, described in period publications as Chicago's "South Union Station," but these were not acted upon. Instead, Dearborn was nominally improved after World War II.

Santa Fe was one of the most important tenants of Dearborn. Its famous trains to and from the West Coast originated and terminated here. The *Chief, Super Chief, El Capitan*, and many other named limiteds began their long journey to the Southwest beneath Dearborn's antique shed. As it were, Santa Fe was the last major tenant. Shortly after Amtrak assumed long-distance passenger service in 1971, it shifted the remaining Santa Fe trains to Union Station.

Although Dearborn was closed to long-distance traffic, Norfolk & Western maintained one platform for its lone Orland Park commuter train until the mid-1970s, when this too was finally shifted to Union Station. The shed was a classic, and a preservation effort was mounted to save it. However, in 1976 Dearborn's train shed was demolished and the area behind the head house was redeveloped.

Dearborn's survival distinguishes it from most of the other major terminals where old station buildings were demolished to make way for modern office towers or other developments, but in some cases the tracks remained active. In the case of Chicago Grand Central, both station and shed, at one time among the finest in the nation, were destroyed and little remains today. Except for a

Interestingly, Dearborn Station was opened a few years prior to completion of its terminal building in 1885. So for a few years in the early 1880s, passengers had to tolerate various temporary station facilities, notably those located at 12th and State Streets.

Once completed, Dearborn's brick station building was in many ways typical of nineteenth-century American

portion of Chicago Union Station, Dearborn is Chicago's only surviving traditional station and the only remaining nineteenth-century railway terminal in the city. The head house was refurbished and adapted for non-rail applications in the 1980s. Today it is something of an attraction and is home to a variety of businesses and retail tenants, including restaurants and bars, a dance school, medical offices, and a shipping business outlet, as well as law offices. Although more than forty years have passed since the last long-distance train departed, Dearborn isn't far from Chicago Union Station and remains within walking distance from the downtown Loop.

DENVER UNION STATION

Denver Union Station is a Beaux Arts, neoclassical, steel-framed granite building. Its iconic "Travel by Train" red neon sign was a later addition. The station has undergone two significant transformations a century apart. The original Denver Union Station was a nineteenth-century Romanesque design that was largely destroyed by fire; it was rebuilt to the design of Taylor, Van Brundt and Howe in 1914. Historically, it was jointly owned by the Burlington, Rio Grande, Rock Island, Santa Fe, and Union Pacific and served some eighty daily trains, mostly long-distance trains connecting far-flung cities. In its heyday it was also served by interurban electric trains. Its traffic was devastated by mid-twentieth-century cuts to passenger services, and, by 1983, it was only serving Amtrak's daily *California Zephyr* and the seasonal *Rio Grande Ski Train*. Its once-busy platforms were only a shadow of former times.

The area around Denver Union at 17th and Wynkoop Streets was rejuvenated and became a popular neighborhood. The station was enhanced by shops and trendy restaurants. Its second transformation into the Union Station Transportation Center was completed in 2014, which included erecting modern canopies over the tracks that augment the appearance of the Beaux Arts main building. It now hosts expanded light-rail services and a new twenty-two-gate bus concourse in addition to Amtrak facilities. A host of new shops, restaurants, a hotel, and related facilities have brought life back to the historic structure. The expected inaugural of the new East Rail commuter rail/airport service to the Denver International Airport in 2016, among other planned suburban rail routes, will contribute to the old Union Station's revitalized role as a significant railway transportation hub.

PHILADELPHIA'S READING TERMINAL

Philadelphia & Reading thrived in the late nineteenth century by dominating the anthracite territory in eastern Pennsylvania. For Reading, hard coal really was "black diamonds"; the railroad was among the richest of its day. To display its wealth, it built an ornately decorated company headquarters and passenger terminal on Philadelphia Center City's Market Street thoroughfare.

Reading Terminal was built to the architectural pattern perfected by London's St. Pancras station (see Chapter 5), using two distinct structures for the head house and train shed. New York Architect F. H. Kimball designed the nine-story Italianate-style head house—faced with pink and white granite and decorated with terra-cotta trim—that largely housed railroad offices.

This vintage postcard portrays Philadelphia's Reading Terminal as it appeared in its heyday. Centrally located facing Market Street, this massive station was designed for the prosperous Philadelphia & Reading Railroad in an Italian Renaissance style by New York architect Francis Harry Kimball. Completed in 1893, it served as a passenger terminal until November 1984. Located below the old shed, Reading Terminal Market still thrives after more than 115 years. *Sean Solomon collection*

Behind the head house is an enormous balloon-style train shed designed and built by Philadelphia's Wilson Brothers.

Reading Terminal operated as the downtown passenger station for ninety-one years. During the 1930s, Reading electrified its busy suburban operations. The railroad's story is one from riches to rags. Once the pride of the industry and one of America's finest lines, Reading suffered terribly as anthracite fell out of fashion; by the 1970s, Reading was bankrupt. In 1976, the railroad was included in the Conrail bailout aimed at salvaging the operation of a half-dozen ailing Eastern carriers.

By this time, the South Eastern Pennsylvania Transportation Authority (SEPTA) had been subsidizing Philadelphia commuter rail for several years, and in its final period as a passenger station, Reading Terminal strictly served SEPTA suburban trains. Consolidation of Philadelphia's suburban services in the mid-1980s linked the former Pennsylvania Railroad Suburban station a few blocks to the west with former Reading Company routes via a new tunnel. This included a new four-track underground station called Market East (since renamed Jefferson Station), resulting in the closure of Reading Terminal in 1984.

Yet the old station building and train shed survive. Today the Reading Terminal shed is the last surviving example of a balloon-style train shed in North America. Although the tracks were removed, the shed and station were renovated in the mid-1990s and reopened as part of a convention center in 1998.

The station's Market Street façade looks more or less the same as it always has. Inside, modern trappings have

Murals at Reading Terminal give a hint of what it would have been like under the shed in the steam era: a classic anthracite burning "Camelback" is front and center, while Reading Company's stainless-steel *Crusader* on at the right. Back in the day the streamlined *Crusader* connected Philadelphia and Central Railroad of Jersey's Jersey City Terminal (where passengers could catch a ferry to lower Manhattan). *Brian Solomon*

largely replaced traditional railway station décor. Today, escalators whisk visitors to the level once occupied by tracks, and the vast space beneath the shed is available as a convention hall, brightly lit with polished floors. A mural opposite the shed portrays the station as it looked in the days of steam, featuring an image of Reading Company's famed Budd-built, steam-hauled, stainless-steel streamliner, the *Crusader*. Budd was a railway car manufacturer and, like the Reading Company, was Philadelphia-based, so the portrayal of the *Crusader* has special significance.

One of the few elements of the old order that has survived is the Reading Terminal Market located below the shed, which dates from the opening of the station in 1893. The market retains a link to the old Reading Company through its classic diamond-shaped logo, which emulates the logo historically used by the railroad. Vendors sell everything from freshly prepared food—including fresh bread, fish, and imported cheeses—to flowers, candles, and scented potpourri. At Christmastime an O-gauge Lionel model railroad is set up to entertain children.

5 OVERSEAS WONDERS

RAILWAY NETWORKS IN GREAT BRITAIN AND EUROPE

developed differently than in America. In the early days of the railways, the United States and the British colony that became Canada were new countries with underdeveloped infrastructure and lightly populated cities and towns. Road networks, where they existed, tended to be primitive and poorly constructed. As a result, North America was ripe for railway development, with new corridors of commerce encouraging and focusing new settlement.

Many towns and cities, especially in the Midwest and Western states and provinces, owe their very existence to the coming of the railroad. By contrast, European nations were already well settled; towns and cities were long established and in some cases already densely populated. Road networks had been around for centuries, as well as inland navigation systems comprised of rivers and shipping canals. So when railways were built in Europe they tended to connect existing population centers.

Planning and growth of railways followed different objectives. From the beginning, many American railroads were viewed as the domain of private enterprise. While a few lines, such as the Western Railroad (of Massachusetts) and early transcontinental ventures, benefited from government planning and investment, these were the notable exceptions. Most North American railroads were conceived and built as privately operated profit-making businesses. A focus on operating profitably dictated where routes were established, while competition between companies frequently resulted in duplicative lines and overlapping infrastructure. Important towns would often have three

Irish Rail's Kent Station in Cork features an unusual train shed located on an exceptionally tight curve. This is a function of its location, which is tightly placed between a long tunnel on the Dublin end and the Cork waterfront. *Brian Solomon*

There is perhaps no finer link between railways and the visual arts than the Musée' d'Orsay in Paris. It was built between 1897 and 1900 as the Gare d'Orsay from the enlightened designs of Parisian architect Victor Laloux—well known as a professor at the influential École des Beaux-Arts. Its construction coincided with the Paris Exposition of 1900. In the early 1980s, it was transformed into *Musée' du XIXe* (Museum of the Nineteenth Century) and is universally known as the Musée' d'Orsay. *Brian Solomon*

or four companies competing for traffic, each with their own stations, yards, and branches.

By contrast, European lines and those in many countries around the world were often national projects, planned by national governments. Certainly in many situations, private companies were involved, typically in railway construction and supply, and sometimes in operation, but route planning and line location was more strictly controlled by the government. As a result, with some notable exceptions (such as in London and Paris),

there were fewer instances of duplicative infrastructure in Europe and less point-to-point competition. Railway lines were viewed from the beginning as national infrastructure, and construction tended to be both adequately funded and highly engineered. Yet, each nation followed a different model, leading to considerable variation in strategy. In some countries, railways were begun as strictly state-sponsored projects. In others, there were varying degrees of private ownership and private operation, and in some instances operations vacillated between public and private models depending on moods and demands of the times.

Since European railways tended to serve established population centers and benefited from public planning and more generous funding, these railways were quicker to develop impressive architecture. This was especially true in the largest cities, where the notion of a city gate was established. As the value of railways gained both momentum and traffic, the demands for large city stations produced some outstanding examples of railway engineering.

Britain, in particular, set many groundbreaking precedents. Not only did Britain originate much of the basic railway technology, such as the steam locomotive, but it established the world's first public railways; these examples were soon mimicked around the world. America was first to adopt British railway technology, and early American railways imported both technology and know-how across the Atlantic.

The very concept of a railway station was a British innovation, both in its refinement of the small country station and with large city terminals. Britain's stations were emulated in America, across its far-flung empire, on the Continent, and elsewhere around the world. When studying the great railway stations, the astute student of railways naturally looks toward Great Britain and British-built railways across its empire.

Thankfully, Britain also has had a great appreciation for its heritage, and despite economic changes, development, advancement of more modern transportation systems, and draconian scaling back of its own railway network, Britain has maintained and preserved many of its classic railway stations. Today, we can step back more than a century and study great architectural works, some of which have been preserved like working fossils, while others have been cleverly integrated into modern transport centers.

Above: Normally Dublin's Heuston Station is a beehive of activity, but all was quiet on Christmas Day 2004. Irish Rail and Dublin Bus do not operate on this holiday. Originally called Kingsbridge Station, named for the nearby span over the River Liffey, this was one of several Irish railway stations renamed in 1966 for heroes of the 1916 Easter Rising. Sean Heuston was among the Irish patriots captured by British authorities and executed on May 8, 1916, at the Kilmainham Gaol (jail) just a short walk from the railway terminal. *Brian Solomon*

Left: Dublin's Heuston Station is one of the world's oldest big city railway terminals in continuous use. Its traditional booking hall, as seen in this January 12, 2005, photograph, features a period clerestory ceiling with ornate molding. This was the original entrance for the terminal, while the impressive building at the front of the station was actually the Great Southern & Western Railway offices. *Brian Solomon*

There are only a few days during the year when the rays of setting sun reach deep into the recesses of Heuston Station's Victorian-era train shed. The design of the shed and principal members including cast-iron columns date to the 1840s, while much of the overhead material was replaced during extensive restoration during 2005 and 2006. *Brian Solomon*

HISTORIC ARCHITECTURE AND MODERN NETWORKS

Among the distinct differences between contemporary North American and European railway networks are fundamentally different emphases. In North America, privately operated railroads have focused on the most lucrative aspects of their businesses. As competition developed during the twentieth century, they gradually lost localized high-value freight and passenger businesses. Instead, railways gradually refocused into carriers of long-distance, high-volume bulk freight, moving whole trainloads of coal, oil, grain, and containers. Passenger services declined in importance after World War I, and passenger volumes dropped off rapidly after World War II. With

a few exceptions, North America's private railroads effectively stopped investing in passenger facilities by the mid-1940s and bought their last new passenger equipment in the 1950s.

Remaining passenger services were conveyed to government subsidized operators during the 1970s and 1980s. In the United States, Amtrak assumed responsibility for most remaining long-distance services in 1971. Various commuter-rail operators were established from the 1960s to the 1980s, with a host of new commuter systems emerging since the 1990s. During the long decline, many traditional railroad station buildings were converted to other railroad purposes, sold to third parties, or demolished. While Americans have expressed renewed enthusiasm for passenger trains, especially in the Northeast and California, nationally the level of passenger services are just a fraction of what were operated seventy years ago.

European railways followed a different path. Across continental Europe, intercity services were sustained and expanded after World War II. Although railways

Above: Poland's railway routes were largely built before the Polish state was reestablished following World War I. Historically, Warsaw was ringed by railway terminals; Vienna Station served trains running toward both Vienna and Berlin; Vistula Station hosted trains running north toward Danzig (now Gdánsk); while St. Petersburg Station focused on that named Russian city, and trains to the east served Terespol Station. Warszawa Centralna (Warsaw Central), pictured here, is a Soviet-era construction built in the massive concrete style characteristic of the period and completed in 1975. The main waiting room is above ground, but trains are accessed via four underground platforms. *Brian Solomon*

Below: Although Glasgow Central station opened in 1879, its shed wasn't completed until 1882. Increased traffic warranted additional platforms that were built in the late 1880s. This view was exposed in February 1998. *Brian Solomon*

lost market share to automobiles and airlines, there has been continued investment in national railway networks, with growth resulting from increased populations and the desire for greater mobility. Advancements, notably development of true high-speed railway services, such as the French TGV that now can travel at speeds in excess of 200 miles per hour on select routes, have maintained high intercity ridership across much of Europe. In some nations, branch lines have been cut back; in others, such as Belgium, Germany, Slovenia, and Switzerland, secondary lines have continued to serve as feeders and are viewed as necessary means of rural development.

In part stemming from a long architectural tradition dating back to antiquity, European railways viewed stations from their early days as warranting architectural significance. Across Britain and the Continent great stations have resulted in a blend of classic railway architecture with convenience. In more modern times, the heritage of traditional stations has been preserved, even when old structures are expanded, while new railway lines and new structures have continued to augment historic infrastructure with innovative architectural styles. State-of-the-art, high-speed trains gliding beneath cavernous Victorian-era train sheds make for a wonderful historic contrast. Across the Continent it is possible to avoid the stress associated with airline and automotive travel. The ability to board a fast train in the traditional city center and travel hassle-free is one of the great pleasures of continental Europe. Not only is this easier on the individual traveler, but since railway travel requires less energy than by either road or air, it lowers the railway traveler's carbon footprint. Electrification is widespread across the Continent, and most major routes benefit from the greater efficiency and acceleration offered by electrically powered trains.

Urban centers have maintained their historic vitality in part because of excellent intercity and suburban railway services and their equivalent transit connections that enable travelers to easily switch between modes at urban hubs. Modern advances have offered new solutions. Germany pioneered the concept of the "tram-train," enabling previously unprecedented transportation flexibility by running streetcars on the same tracks as intercity services. This was first applied in Karlsruhe where trams operate directly into the main station and continue on suburban routes using a mix of tramline and mainline trackage.

France has undergone a light-rail renaissance with

some two dozen cities adopting innovative light-rail networks with trams traversing a mix of city streets, private rights of way, and subway lines.

Massive railway infrastructure projects in the past few decades have made significant improvement to the European railway network, unlike in America where the railway route structure effectively stopped growing in the 1920s and the majority of the lines date to routes planned in the nineteenth century. Italy, France, and later Germany led the way in building all-new, specially engineered high-speed lines. In recent years, all-new high-speed routes have been built in Belgium and

Holland. Today Spain has one of the most impressive high-speed networks, with new lines radiating across the country from the capital, Madrid.

Switzerland has invested in construction of lengthy trans-alpine tunnels aimed at increasing the capacity of their national network while simultaneously improving its overall efficiency.

Among the most intriguing railway projects has been completion of the Channel Tunnel between Britain and France, which has facilitated high-speed service directly between London and both Paris and Brussels. Today, passengers can board sleek *Eurostar* trains at London's

In 1981, the introduction of high-speed rail service between the historic Paris Gare de Lyon terminus and the southern city of Lyon inspired a rail renaissance in France and across the continent. In this June 2012 view, modern Alsthom-designed TGV trains wait for passengers beneath the mid-nineteenth century iron shed that once protected steam locomotives of the old Compagnie des chemins de fer de Paris à Lyon et à la Méditerranée, best known by its initials PLM—one of six historic French regional railways. *Tim Doherty*

Above: Spain operates some of the world's fastest trains. The Iberian high-speed revolution began in 1990s, with the import of the French high-speed system and initially used custom-styled TGV-like trains—marketed as *Alta Velocidad Española* (AVE). Some of the most recent lines allow top speeds in excess of 200 miles per hour. Some of the original AVE high-speed train sets rest under the shed at purpose-built terminus in Sevilla (Seville). *Brian Solomon*

Right top: Using a blend of neoclassic and rationalist architecture, Jacob Hittorf designed the station at Paris Gare du Nord to serve as a suitable entrance to the French capital. Built between 1861 and 1864, the station is still used today and is one of six traditional terminals that ring Paris. *Brian Solomon*

Right bottom: From steam locomotives to high-speed electric trains, the shed at Paris Gare du Nord has seen a century-and-a-half of change. It makes for a wonderful contrast in time periods. The station's builders would have been delighted to learn that by 1994 through service would commence between Paris and London through an undersea tunnel using French-built train sets. *Brian Solomon*

Victorian-era St. Pancras station (detailed below) and travel at speeds up to 186 miles per hour to arrive under the shed at Paris Gare du Nord in just two hours. In that amount of time, an air traveler would have barely enough time to travel in traffic from central London to Heathrow and to pass through the various levels of security and related boarding procedures. And, since the end of the Soviet domination of eastern Europe, many rail links have been reestablished between eastern and western European nations.

Yet, other elements of European railway travel have declined. The recent proliferation of cheap airlines and high-speed rail links have all but killed traditional overnight train travel. In recent years, the network of international sleeping car trains has suffered continual decline. Where only a couple of decades ago, long trains of sleeping cars rolled overnight between major European cities, today only a few trains remain. Likewise, traditional locomotive-hauled trains with windows that open and compartmentalized carriages have given way to open-seating arrangements with sealed windows and climate control.

LONDON STATIONS

London was the primary focus of many British railways, and no city in the world boasted more terminals. Before Dr. Richard Beeching's report in the early 1960s inspired the draconian consolidation and scaling back of the British railway network, London was ringed by fourteen railway terminals. Despite drastic cuts to the network outside of the London area, most London termini have survived, although only some of them retain their original Victorian architecture.

Today, London's railways are among the busiest in Europe, saturated with a continual parade of passenger trains. Of London's major termini, several are world famous, including Victoria, Paddington, and Waterloo stations. Thanks to the Harry Potter novels and films, one of the best-known stations in London is Kings Cross, a terminal that now features a platform 9 3/4, as highlighted in the stories, for the benefit of visiting tourists.

Although a relative minor player in regard to traffic volume, London's St. Pancras station features one of the most impressive station head houses ever built and one of the world's most influential train sheds. The station building was integrated with the Midland Grand Hotel that was the masterly creation of Sir George Gilbert Scott (1811–1878), built by Midland Railway between 1865 and 1876. It is situated near central London along Euston Road adjacent to Kings Cross. Born at Gawcott, Buckinghamshire, Scott was among the most highly regarded of London's Victorian architects. He began his career as an architectural apprentice and was involved in the design of various ecclesiastical structures; his interest in the Gothic style stemmed from this early experience. He took to heart the opinions of author A. W. N. Pugin on medieval architecture and established himself as a major proponent of the Gothic Revival, working in fourteenth-century Germanic styles.

With St. Pancras station's Midland Grand Hotel, Scott created an imposing and exceptionally ornate brick and stone building, considered exemplary of secular High Victorian Gothic architecture. Its frontal façade rises a full four stories, topped with a steeply pitched

Above: Sir George Gilbert Scott—one of London's best regarded nineteenth-century architects—designed the St. Pancras Station head house, which originally served as the Midland Grand Hotel. This impressive ornate brick-and-stone structure is a premier example of the British secular Victorian Gothic style. *Brian Solomon*

Below: The Midland Grand Hotel at the front of London's St. Pancras Station opened in 1873. When completed, it offered rooms for 500 guests. Although one of London's most elegant Victorian-era railway hotels, times changed and, in 1935, the hotel was converted into railway company offices. It remains one of England's most iconic railway buildings and one of the greatest examples of railway station architecture. *Brian Solomon*

Although the St. Pancras head house garners greater public attention, it is really the great shed that proved to be the most influential part of the station. This was the work of the Midland Railway's engineer William Barlow. Even in the 1860s, London real estate was too valuable to squander and Barlow needed the space below track level for storage. To avoid a complicated network of multi-span shed supports he pioneered the design of a broad and tall balloon-style span that allowed locomotive smoke to escape the station while keeping passengers dry. Today this shed houses St. Pancras International, the terminal for *Eurostar* high-speed trains destined for Paris and Brussels. *Brian Solomon*

roof intensely decorated with gothic dormers, and culminating with an exquisitely executed clock tower.

Beyond Scott's masterful High Gothic Station is St. Pancras' pioneer balloon-arch train shed, featuring an arched roof structure without the need for interior midsection supports. This was the vision of the Midland's engineer, William Barlow, while details of the shed are credited to roof and bridge engineer, R. M. Ordish. It was constructed by the Butterley Company of Derbyshire. This shed remains in daily service, while many of the great sheds it inspired, including Philadelphia's PRR Broad Street Station, have been gone for decades.

Yet, like Broad Street, St. Pancras faced the specter of demolition. Despite Beeching-era efforts to erase Scott's gothic masterpiece, St. Pancras and the old Grand Midland Hotel (which had served as offices since

the 1930s) survived. Since the mid-1990s, it enjoyed a renaissance in part as the result of the reprivatization of British Rail and opening of the Channel Tunnel.

Following privatization, St. Pancras became the terminal for the Midland Mainline franchise. By that time, the station was a grimy relic and its shed a haunting cavernous reminder of another era, its many skylights having been covered over during World War II. Initially, *Eurostar* trains were routed to a temporary International Terminal at Waterloo Station, while plans to transform St. Pancras were set in motion in conjunction with the construction of the Channel Tunnel Rail Link—all new high-speed lines linking London with the west portal of the Channel Tunnel at Folkstone.

Coincident with these improvements, the Midland franchise was won by East Midland Trains, a rail service

Above: Great Western Railway's original Paddington station opened in 1838, but by the early 1850s it required a better London terminal. GWR's legendary mastermind Isambard K. Brunel participated in the design of this grand new station. Brunel's sheds date from about 1853; however, as traffic grew, Paddington Station was modified and expanded. Additional sheds were built in the early twentieth century to match Brunel's design, while the station was expanded again between 1930 and 1934. *Tim Doherty*

Below: The Great Central Railway was the last major mainline to reach London. Its terminus at Marylebone, completed in the late 1890s, was considered the final classic London terminal station. Some critics have dismissed it because it was not built to the same grand style as other of the London stations; instead of hiring a famous architect, Great Central stooped to allowing their own engineering department to do the design work. Great Central's H. W. Broddock is credited with its finer details. Today this station is largely used for suburban traffic as most of Great Central's long-distance routes were rationalized as result of Dr. Richard Beeching's recommendations in the 1960s. *Brian Solomon*

Opposite: The opulent station at L'viv, Ukraine, could be easily mistaken for a royal palace; it is among Europe's finest railway terminals. L'viv is a moderate-sized city in western Ukraine. An awful lot has changed in just 100 years; a century ago the city was called Lemberg and served as a provincial capital in the Hapsburg's far-flung empire. Had a certain Austrian archduke remained in Vienna in 1914, Austrian Federal Railways might serve this station today instead of the Ukrainian Railways. *Brian Solomon*

Below: The Polish city of Wrocław has a long and complicated history owing to many border changes in central Europe over the centuries. When its railroads were constructed in the mid-nineteenth century, the city was located within German territory and known as Breslau. After World War II, it became part of the modern Polish state. Wrocław Główny, the city's main railway terminal, serves lines radiating in every direction. The station building was designed to resemble a medieval castle. *Brian Solomon*

operated by the Stagecoach Group, which contributed to an expansion of domestic long-distance service from St. Pancras. In addition, a new underground station for electric suburban trains operated by First Capitol Connect was built below the main station. Previously, suburban passengers used a cramped Thames Link station (now closed) located to the south of Euston Road.

St. Pancras was modernized, its classic train shed was renewed and iron work painted a sky blue, while the bottom of the station, originally designed for storage, was opened for public use as a shopping plaza, food court, and concourse. This made the already capacious interior seem even larger. Among the changes was construction of a shed extension that was long enough to accommodate eighteen-car-long *Eurostar* trains. Modern designers decided not to emulate Barlow's Victorian ironwork, so the new shed augments the station in ways that nineteenth-century passengers couldn't have imagined. The renewed station opened with great celebration in 2007.

In 2006, Berlin's long-anticipated Hauptbahnhof (Central station) opened on Invalidenstrasse. This modern station features noise and vibration suppression systems to minimize the effects of passing trains. Like traditional big-city railway terminals, it offers passengers a variety of services,

shops, and restaurants. Trains depart in every direction from this hub, which is now among the most important in Germany and one of the busiest in Europe. An InterCity train led by a class 101 electric pauses at the Berlin Hbf in July 2013. *Tim Doherty*

HAUPTBAHNHOFS— GERMAN CENTRAL STATIONS

In 1879, the construction of the Hanover Hauptbahnhof (meaning *main* or *central* station and abbreviated "Hbf") set a precedent for similar centralized railway terminals at other large German cities. Frankfurt Hbf, a large stub-end terminal completed in 1888 after nearly a decade of construction, features a vast three-span balloon shed.

Today, Frankfurt Hbf remains one of Germany's busiest, and its vast nineteenth-century sheds provide a contrast with the modern ICE3 high-speed trains that glide in and out on regular intervals. The maze of trackage serving the Frankfurt Hbf is impressive. Multiple approaches with parallel sets of crossovers allow for parallel train movements in and out of the station.

In 1907, Leipzig began construction of a massive new Haupbahnhof (main central station) to consolidate facilities from a number of older terminals to provide passengers with a better, more convenient station. The Haupbahnhof was built on the site of Leipzig's Thüringer Bahnhöfe near the Sachsenplatz at the heart of the city center. The expansive new railway building featured a vast three-tiered roof designed to conceal the train sheds behind it. For many years it was the largest, if not the busiest, station in Europe. *Period postcard, Solomon collection*

Köln's was among the most unusual of the large terminal designs by using a unified station and shed design. Booking offices, waiting rooms, and other station facilities are located beneath the shed rather than adjacent to it. While this might seem strange, in the 1890s when the Köln (Cologne) Hauptbahnhof was built, this style of shed-only stations had emerged as a preferred German arrangement.

Köln's through station has a full set of approach tracks at both ends, and yet it is also a main terminal—an exceptionally busy one at that. The station's long balloon shed is adjacent to Köln's monumental gothic cathedral. The station, cathedral and bridge over the Rhine were all badly damaged by Allied bombing raids during World War II and required massive reconstruction after the war.

Classic German terminal construction reached its zenith with completion of the Hamburg Hauptbahnhof in 1906, and the even more expansive Leipzig Hauptbahnhof that began construction in 1907 and opened on the eve of World War I (although not completed until 1915). This conveniently located main station is situated opposite Leipzig's Sachsenplatz, where it replaced the city's old Thüringer Bahnhof.

Leipzig — *Der neue Hauptbahnhof.*

Der neue Hauptbahnhof in Leipzig ist der größte Bahnhof Europas. Es münden 26 Geleise nebeneinander ein. Im Jahre 1902 wurde mit den Bauten begonnen. Die linke Hälfte (preußischer Teil) ist seit 1. Mai 1912 vollständig im Betrieb und von der anderen Hälfte der sächsische Teil seit 1. Februar 1913 teilweise. Die vollständige Inbetriebnahme erfolgt 1915. Von den Gesamtkosten — ca. 150 Millionen — trägt der sächsische Staat 50 Millionen und die Stadt Leipzig ca. 17 Millionen Mark.

At the time of construction, Leipzig Hbf was the most expensive station in Europe, and the city itself paid for roughly one-third of the cost of the terminal building. The design of its head house is credited to Dresden architects William Lossow and Max Hans Kühne. This is an unusually broad building, with nearly 1,000 feet of frontage. Inside is a spacious passenger concourse.

Leipzig's shed was designed by engineers Eiler & Karing and used six-spans to cover twenty-six tracks with thirteen broad platforms between them. It is noticeably lower and brighter than vast balloon-style sheds of Germany's earlier large stations. Author John A. Droege was impressed by the station's sheer size, and in *Passenger Terminals and Trains* (1975) he noted that the entire station occupied an estimated 882,642 square feet. During the postwar years, the Soviet socialist economy of the German Democratic Republic allowed the Leipzig

Germany's Köln Hauptbahnhof features an unusual design; the station is below the shed rather than adjacent to it. To the east of the station is the massive Hohenzollern Bridge. This was constructed between 1907 and 1911. Not far from the Köln Hauptbahnhof is the city's famous Dom, the city's immense Gothic cathedral. The station, bridge, and cathedral were badly damaged during bombing raids in World War II. The bridge was reconstructed with six tracks and today is an exceptionally busy span with a continual parade of passenger trains feeding the station. An InterCity Express is seen arriving at Köln under the modern extension to the original balloon-style shed; the bridge is visible in the distance to the left. *Tim Doherty*

Hbf to deteriorate into a dark grimy shadow. Following German reunification in 1990, it was restored.

The Stuttgart Hbf was begun prior to World War I but not finished until the interwar period. This station's massive blockish simplicity offers a contrast to the neoclassical styles of other early-twentieth-century German stations.

PRAGUE HLAVNI NÁDRAŽÍ

Visitors to the Czech capital may be forgiven if they pass by Hlavni Nádraží (main railway station), even if they arrive by train. Prague is a city well known for its world-class architecture and fortunate to have been spared from widespread and catastrophic damage suffered by many European cities during the World Wars. Prague Hlavni Nádraží is significant as a rare example of a large city station designed in the Art Nouveau style. In any other city, that station's distinctive architecture would have marked it as a notable civic structure. However, it is lost in a city of architectural wonders and, even in contemporary railway literature, the station is rarely mentioned.

Prague, like many cities in central Europe, has a complicated history. Over the centuries, political boundaries have changed many times and often were considerably different than today. For centuries, the Hapsburg dynasty was one of the leading powers in Europe. For nearly 400 years, from 1526 to 1918, Prague was under Hapsburg rule, serving as the capital of Bohemia. In the nineteenth century, Prague industrialized and was connected by railway lines to key cities across the Hapsburg's Austro-Hungarian empire.

Czech nationalism took hold during this period. Then, in 1918, following the defeat of the empire at the end of World War I, Prague was established as the capital of the newly created Czechoslovakia, one of several new nations carved out of former Austro-Hungarian territory.

The original railway building dates to 1871, when it was known as Prague Kaiser Franz Josef Bahnhof (Emperor Franz Joseph Station). Between 1901 and 1909, the head house was substantially remodeled to the design of Czech architect Joseph Fanta (1856–1954), one of the leading Czech proponents of the Art Nouveau movement.

This relatively short-lived architectural style originated in Belgium in the 1890s with architects Victor

Opposite: Years of neglect had left Prague's once beautiful Hlavni Nádrazi dirty and poorly maintained. Sadly for many passengers, all they saw of the station was the heavily stained metal shed. From here they were generally directed into Soviet-era additions and tended to miss the finer area of the old station building. *Brian Solomon*

Right above: Prague's Hlavni Nádrazi has one of the most elaborately decorated interiors of any railway station in Europe. This central domed area once served as the primary entrance but is now occupied by Fanta's café and is a nod to the station's Czech architect. *Brian Solomon*

Horta (1861–1947) and Paul Hankar (1857–1901). The style was reactionary and aimed to shake the shackles imposed by conventional architectural movements. It embraced curvilinear forms that emulated natural shapes that were made possible by advances in metal work. Interestingly, Art Nouveau appears to have drawn from railway architecture in its early incarnation. In *Space, Time and Architecture*, 5th ed. (2009), author Sigfried Giedion wrote, "What are these lines but the *unrolled* curls and rosettes that are to be under the eaves of so many Belgian railway stations." Ironically, Prague's station remains one of the most prominent examples of Art Nouveau as applied to railway architecture. Other noteworthy examples are stations on the Paris Metro and Helsinki's Main Station (detailed in this chapter).

Fanta's reinterpretation of the Kaiser Franz Josef Bahnhof features a prominent frontal façade characterized by a large frontal archway with curved windows above five entrance doors leading to a vaulted

Helsinki's main station is considered a classic example of Finnish Art Nouveau design. The station's frontal façade is dominated by the great portal archway, which is flanked by pairs of giant globe-wielding statues. Although completed in 1914, events surrounding World War I delayed dedication until 1919, by which time Finland had declared independence from Russia. *Brian Solomon*

main area covered by an elaborately decorated dome. The level of decorative detail lavished on the station has few peers. A varied selection of masks, birds, snakes, and sculpted reliefs cover the building inside and out. These are credited to Czech sculptors Ladislau Šaloun, Stanislau Sucharda, and Cenek Vosmik.

It is these intensive embellishments that help set Prague's station apart from most other European stations. In its main hall, coats of arms representing Berlin, Budapest, Moscow, Paris, Rome, and Vienna infer the connections offered by the station to these major European capitals.

Beyond the main building is a twin span iron and glass shed that covers tracks and platforms. While this makes an impressive array of metalwork, it is not distinctive in its own right but is noteworthy because it has survived intact to the present day. Shortly after exiting the station to the south, the tracks enter a tunnel.

In 1919, Prague main station was renamed Wilsonova Nádraží in honor of American president Woodrow Wilson. The name was dropped after German annexation and occupation during World War II and appears to have been forgotten during the postwar period of Soviet influence that prevailed until the Czechoslovak Velvet Revolution in November 1989. The name change was the least of the station's problems. During this dark period of Czechoslovak history, the station was allowed to deteriorate and by the mid-1990s was a dismal shadow of its former glory.

Complicating matters was construction of a major thoroughfare immediately in front of the station and development of the Prague Metro, which changed the natural flow of passengers in and out of the building while adding hard-edged Soviet-style appendages to the Art Nouveau building. It is because of these late-era alterations that many visitors fail to recognize the station's most interesting features as many passengers are directed off the platforms without ever having an opportunity to experience the station building.

Today Hlavni Nádražĭ is the largest of four main railway stations in Prague and, by one account, the busiest in the Czech Republic. While the special difficulties of the surrounding infrastructure remain a problem, restoration of the structure aimed to correct the years of neglect that began in 2006.

HELSINKI STATION

Perhaps the most famous Art Nouveau railway terminal is Helsingin Päärautatieasema (Helsinki main station), designed by Finnish architect Eliel Saarinen. Constructed between 1911 and 1914 when Finland was under Russian domination, this represents a nationalistic statement through the use of Finnish architectural symbolism. Saarinen melded traditional Finnish themes with themes of the Vienna Secession movement and Arts and Crafts style to deliver a bold architectural statement that has been compared to the nationalistic music in *Finlandia* by composer Jean Sibelius.

Art Nouveau made use of new materials and construction techniques, and so like Fanta's Prague station, Saarinen's Helsinki station helped pioneer the use of reinforced concrete in European station construction. Today this is a common construction technique.

Saarinen's station design is characterized by his use of a large central entrance arch and massive clock tower. Yet the most memorable features are the pairs of masculine stone giants with outstretched arms holding large globes situated on either side of the arch. These, like the outer walls, were constructed from Finnish

For a capital city, Helsinki station is surprisingly convenient. Not only is this station centrally located and represents the city's primary terminal, but the facilities, including tracks and platforms, are situated at ground level. Its three main entrances allow passengers easy access from trains to the city center. Although the outer walls are constructed of typical Finnish granite, the station interior vaults were made from reinforced concrete. *Brian Solomon*

granite. Saarinen's design inspired American architects Fellheimer & Wagner: Compare the views of Saarinen's Helsinki station with the Art Deco–styled stations at Buffalo and Cincinnati featured in Chapter 4. Saarinen designed a similar station at Viipuri (Vyborg), but this was short lived as it was destroyed by Soviet forces during World War II. The city of Vyborg and surrounding territory were reclaimed by the Soviet Union as result of a wartime border change.

In 1913, architect Ulisse Stacchini won the competition for Milan's new Central Station. Although construction didn't begin for another dozen years, his vision for a gargantuan terminal building neatly coincided with Italian Fascist architectural ideals that favored monumental construction to demonstrate the power of the state. Today, the massive station seems out of proportion with humanity; the head house features this enormous colonnade measuring 607 feet long and 90 feet high. *Brian Solomon*

STAZIONE DI MILANO CENTRALE

Stazione di Milano Centrale (Milan Central Station) is a monumental railway terminal that faces the Piazza Duca d'Aosta, one of the largest squares in Europe. Its design was the result of an architectural competition held in Milan in 1913, won by architect Ulisse Stacchini. Although the plan dated from before World War I, its blocky style and super-human scale seems to typify the public architecture of the interwar Fascist period. It was one of the last great railway stations built in Europe before World War II.

Construction of the Milan station faced repeated delays, complicated as a result of difficulties posed by the war and later by the postwar financial distress. Work finally began in 1925, and six years later the station was completed. Stacchini's design embodies neoclassical elements on a gigantic scale and with unusual proportions. Critics have variously described it as "grotesque" and "crushing."

The frontal colonnade has titanic proportions: 607 feet long, 90 feet high, and 79 feet wide, with three huge porticos each of which is 29.5 feet wide and 53 feet high. It provides a vestibule over a roadway used by vehicular traffic serving the station, similar to the arrangement at Washington Union Station. Consistent with the station's style, the entrance hall is also out of scale with human proportions. The hall is faced with Roia Marble and Travertine stone. Vast stairways lead up to the tracks—25 feet above street level—and a vast concourse hosting a shopping arcade.

Milan's sheds were among the last of the large-arch variety, as typified in an earlier era by the balloon style previously described. They were built in Europe and were equally impressive in their capacious covering of the platform area. Of the five spans, the central shed is by far the largest. Ironically, by the time Milan's balloon sheds were built, traditional balloon sheds in America were being dismantled. The platforms are extraordinarily long, reaching beyond the shed to a distance 1,051 feet from the concourse.

Today, the station hosts a variety of local trains and is a hub for long-distance services, including high-speed trains. Outside, connections to the city are provided by trams and lines two and three of the underground metro system.

Left: The stone sculptures decorating Milano Centrale (Milan Central Station) are larger than life and always viewed from considerable distance owning to the great height of the station roof. *Brian Solomon*

Below: Milano Centrale (Milan Central Station) was constructed in the automotive age, and thus features a vast open vestibule 79 feet wide that covers the roadway for automotive traffic serving the station. This is similar lo vestibule arrangements at Washington Union Station and Philadelphia's 30th Street. *Brian Solomon*

MODERN MASTERPIECES

The list of great European, Asian, and Australian stations includes not only classic gems but also a variety of modern masterpieces. Continued investment in railway infrastructure has produced some impressive modern stations. These include completely new stations, such as the long-awaited Berlin Hauptbahnhof that finally opened in 2006 and is now one of the busiest stations on the Continent. Others integrate traditional terminals with expanded modern facilities, such as Antwerpen-Centraal, which blended architect Louis de la Censerie's elaborate and elegantly adorned station building and its spacious balloon-style shed with two modern new levels. The lowest level provides through connections to the north. The original station opened in 1898, while the improved and expanded modern terminal reopened in 2007.

Above: The five great steel arch sheds at Milano Centrale (Milan Central Station) match the super-human proportions established by the head house. These cover the vast platform area and dwarf the trains below; they also represent a late-era architectural anomaly as they were built later than most of the traditional European sheds. *Brian Solomon*

Opposite: Antwerpen Centraal (Antwerp Central Station) is a station that fulfills an idealized view of the European railway terminal as a blend of castle, cathedral, and railway platform. It is an outstandingly opulent transportation facility. In recent years, the historic station, which dates to 1898, was augmented by two modern levels of track, including a new through station on the lowest level. These modern additions, however, did not embrace the same ornate décor as the original station and have more in common with the functionality of an airport. *Brian Solomon*

Spanish architect Santiago Calatrava (born 1951) has designed several inspiring European stations that characterize his open-flowing organic style of architecture. Calatrava, having studied at the former Polytechnic University of Valencia and later at the Swiss Federal Institute of Technology in Zurich, employs both architectural and engineering skills in his buildings. One of his early railway station projects was the TGV station built at the Lyon Airport in France between 1989 and 1994. Perhaps his best-known railway station is Lisbon's Gare do Oriente, a through suburban station on the outskirts of the Portuguese capital. Commissioned in 1993, this was built to coincide with Lisbon's World Expo in 1998. It features an abnormally tall open-air train shed styled to resemble palms at a desert oasis, constructed from steel and glass. Station facilities and a multimodal terminal are located below track level.

Above: Lisbon's Gare do Oriente (Oriente Station) is a multimodal transportation center commissioned in 1993 and designed by Spanish architect-engineer Santiago Calatrava. It was completed in 1998 to coincide with Lisbon's World Expo. Long-distance and suburban trains are served at the top level where canopies made from steel and glass were designed to emulate the appearance of a palm-covered oasis. *Brian Solomon*

Opposite: Nationale Maatschappij der Belgische Spoorwegen/ Société nationale des chemins de fer belges NMBS/SNCB is Belgium's national railway company and operates one of Europe's finest modern integrated railway systems. On September 19, 2009, it opened a stunning modern station at Leige, Belgium's third-largest city, located in the eastern part of the country near the German frontier. This was designed by Spanish architect-engineer Santiago Calatrava to serve a dual purpose of a railway station and a bridge between areas of the city previously divided by the presence of the railway. The enormous vaulted canopy covers five railway platforms. This is a very busy station hosting a range of services from local NMBS/SNCB trains to international high-speed services including the *Thalys* running from Paris to Köln. *Brian Solomon*

Perhaps one of Calatrava's most impressive creations is the new station at Liege, Belgium, opened in 2009, that has the combined function of serving as both a passenger station and as a bridge between the two sides of the city divided by the railway line. This features creative use of space and a tall shed that dwarfs the trains beneath it. Liege station was obviously intended to be admired. Tall open sidewalks on at each end of the station and on the south side make for great platforms to view the station and the continual parade of trains passing though it. In 2013, Calatrava's Stazione di Bologna e Reggio Emilia av Mediopadana has opened on the latest Italian Direttissima (high-speed line) that connects the two highly populated cities of Bologna and Milan.

Above: A suburban train approaches the platforms at Shinjuku Station in Tokyo. *Brian Solomon*

Opposite top: Budapest, like other European capitals, is ringed by railway terminals. Keleti Station has the most impressive architecture, characterized by its enormous fan-shaped window on its main façade. *Brian Solomon*

Opposite bottom: Portuguese stations are famous for elaborate tile decorations. Porto's Sao Bento station building was built in the early twentieth century to plans by architect Marques da Silva. Inside the main hall are elaborate painted-tile murals by Jorge Colaço depicting the history of transportation and events in Portuguese history. *Brian Solomon*

JAPAN

Japan was a comparative latecomer to railways, a full half-century behind developments in Great Britain. Author/photographer Naotaka Hirota paints this romantic vision at the dawn of Japan's railway age in his gorgeously photographed book *The Lure of Japan's Railways* (1969):

> On October 14, 1872, under clear autumn skies, Japan's first railroad service was inaugurated in grand ceremonies held in the presence of Emperor Meiji at two sites—the terminal buildings at Shimbashi, Tokyo and at Yokohama.

> At Tokyo, the Japanese capital, a stately terminal was constructed in 1882. This was described in Ernest F. Carter's *Famous Railway Stations of the World—and Their Traffic* (1958), as the "Grand Tokio Station" *(sic)*. Rapid growth necessitated its replacement in 1914 with a "simple yet imposing structure of brick and granite with a façade over one-fifth of a mile in length." This featured a distinctive hexagonal dome. Unfortunately, it was largely destroyed by bombing during World War II (known in Japan as "The Pacific War").

 By the 1950s, Japanese stations were characterized by functional design built largely from steel and reinforced concrete. In 1964, Japan stunned the world by opening the first of its purpose-built Shinkansen—the all-new, high-speed railway described in the western media as the "Bullet Train." In 1968, Japan National Railways, including its Shinkansen, carried 7 billion passengers annually, yet this was less than half the total national ridership, as private and local railways carried another 9 billion. Continued expansion of the Shinkansen system was an improvement mandated both by the need for improved travel times and the demand to increase the volume of service between the largest cities. Maximum train speed limits were gradually raised to 186 miles per hour on select lines, while the frequency of trains has approached 15 runs an hour in each direction between the busiest cities.

An express blitzes Shizuoka station on the New Tokaido Shinkansen line. Most Shinkansen stations use a simple track arrangement with platforms served by controlled sidings and mainline tracks at the center. This allows stopping trains to get out of the way of expresses while requiring a minimum of infrastructure. *Brian Solomon*

Tokyo's Yamanote Loop is an exceptionally busy suburban line and its stations are designed for a high volume of traffic. *Brian Solomon*

Today, Japan benefits from one of the world's most heavily traveled railway networks and is characterized by some of the densest construction and most frequent operation. The majority of Japanese lines were built as narrow gauge (3 foot 6 inch/1,067mm track width), while Japan's famous high-speed Shinkansen (bullet train route) uses the more conventional 4 foot 8.5 inch track width.

Compared to Europe and North America, Japan has few large stub-end terminals. In Tokyo and Osaka, the most heavily used suburban services focus on using circular loop lines, which keep trains moving through the urban centers while serving multiple stations. Best known is Tokyo's Yamanote Line or "Yamanote Loop." The Shinkansen uses stub-end terminals at end points yet features carefully honed operating practices that require only simplified route structure, owing to a limited number of end destinations that demand rapid terminal turnaround and use remote staging yards. This obviates the need for expansive city-center terminals with dozens of tracks and complex approaches with numerous switches.

The Shikansen network represents only about 10 percent of Japanese railway routes and consists of straightforward high-speed double-track lines that feature expensive highly engineered railway infrastructure that allows for exclusive operation of exceptionally fast passenger trains.

Busy Japanese stations feature modern, functional architecture designed to accommodate vast numbers of passengers. Jeffery Richards and John M. MacKenzie wrote in *The Railway Station: A Social History* (1986) that few old stations survive: "Their architecture has faded into unremarkable modernism, devoted to speed, rush and disciplined circulation." Some exceptions to this extreme architectural utilitarianism can be found at Tokyo's Central and Ueno Stations, which, despite heavy traffic, still feature a sedate neoclassical inspired architecture and a mix of through and stub-end platforms.

Some smaller stations use more colorful architecture. For example, the town of Shimobe is a mountain resort that features a distinctive station that emulates a pagoda. Extensive private railways in Japan, many of which are operated similar to the old North American electric interurbans, tend to feature stub-end terminals in the larger cities since they often serve just two or three points as commuter lines.

Tokyo's Shinjuku Station is one of the world's busiest in terms of traffic; hundreds of trains handle an estimated 3 million daily passengers, many of whom ride through the station en route to other destinations. Unlike traditional railway stations, Shinjuku is a modern facility that doesn't feature distinctive exterior railway architecture. Instead, its station facilities are blended with the surrounding shopping plazas and department stores with tracks and platforms below. There are twenty through tracks served by ten platforms for mainline trains plus additional tracks, platforms, and facilities for rapid-transit connections. At peak times the station seems like a seething sea of humanity.

AUSTRALIA

Australia's earliest steam railway was the Melbourne & Hobson's Bay Railway Company. In the 1850s, this privately funded enterprise founded the core of a suburban railway on its namesake Victoria metropolis with a terminal at Flinders Street that opened on September 12, 1854. *The Argus* (Melbourne's daily newspaper) recorded this historic event, which was reprinted in Brian Carroll's *Australia's Railway Days* (1976): "Long before the hour appointed—twelve o'clock—a great crowd assembled around the station, the Melbourne terminus, line the whole southern side of Flinders Street, from the station to the Wharf."

Flinders Street was the nexus for a developing passenger network. Tracks ran parallel to the street and the Yarra River. As the station evolved, its arrangement with long platforms was a function of this confining geography.

The original company was absorbed by the Victorian Railways in the 1870s, which facilitated further growth of suburban passenger lines. At that time, the station had grown to three platforms. By the end of the nineteenth century, the volume of traffic had outpaced the capacity of the old terminal while public expectations demanded more elaborate facilities on par with great railway stations in other cities.

Early in the twentieth century, a grand new station was planned and built in the glamorous French Renaissance style. The main building rose three stories tall and ran along Flinders Street between Elizabeth and Swanston Streets. A suitably impressive entrance on the corner of Flinders and Swanston was capped with an impressive copper dome and adorned with clocks. The station became a Melbourne icon and remained key to its public transport infrastructure.

As traffic continued to grow, modern means of facilitating greater numbers of train movements were considered. As early as the 1890s, electrification was explored. In fact, General Electric, the American pioneer of heavy-railroad electrified projects, was initially consulted regarding wiring of suburban services. More than a decade passed before serious action was taken, and in December 1912, electrification of Flinders Street and Melbourne's suburban lines was formally authorized. Interruptions caused by World War I delayed inauguration of electric services until May 1919.

Traffic continued to swell, and by 1958 the station was among the world's busiest railway terminals. Ernest F. Carter reported that Flinders Street accommodated 1,000 passengers per minute at rush hours and as many as 373,000 passengers daily. Several of the world's largest signal control towers accommodate the movement of trains coming in and out of the terminal.

Flinders Street Station is a Melbourne icon and a hub for the city's suburban transport system. © *David Moore / Victoria / Alamy*

To relieve the demands on Flinders Street and to better provide for Melbourne's suburban passengers, an underground city loop line was constructed to augment the traditional terminal. This included construction of three new downtown stations: Parliament, Central, and Flagstaff.

Flinders Street terminal buildings have suffered declines since their heyday. By 2014, the old ballroom and gymnasium that had once been prominent features of the station in its halcyon days were closed off and no longer accessible to the public. However a multimillion-dollar restoration of the building is now in the works and will hopefully return the station to its former glory.

MALAYSIA

Kuala Lumpur, the capitol of Malaysia with a name that translates to "a meeting of muddy waters" or "muddy confluence," is the focus of passenger operations for Keretapi Tanah Melayu Berhad (known by initials KTMB)—the Malayan Railway operator.

Kuala Lumpur's large ornately adorned station has served as a hub for both suburban and long-distance international trains (linking Bangkok, Thailand, and Singapore at the southern frontier of Malaysia). Ernest F. Carter described the station as "looking like a temple with its yellow walls and mosque-like minarets." It was among the most distinctive railway stations in the world,

yet its architecture was in the style of many buildings in Kuala Lumpur. The building was designed by British architect and brigadier General Arthur Benison Hubback and completed before World War I to supplant an earlier building. Despite its unusual style, it shares functional qualities with British colonial railway development elsewhere in the world.

The old station was relieved of its railway functions in 2001 when the new KL Sentral Station opened as the city's principal multimodal hub for heavy rail, monorail, and bus operations. The old station is now a museum and remains as a tourist attraction owning to its distinctive architecture and landmark status.

Above: The Kuala Lumpur historic station is the design of colonial British architect and brigadier General Arthur Benison Hubback. It was built before World War I to serve Britian's colonial railway. Although its styling is exotic, the layout and function of the building is consistent with standard British railway practices.

Above left: Melbourne's Flinders Street Station is the city's main suburban terminal and one of the few large historic railway stations in Australia. Its impressive entrance on the corner of Flinders and Swanston is capped with an impressive copper dome and adorned with clocks. © *Hemis / Alamy*

BIBLIOGRAPHY

BOOKS

1846–1896 Fiftieth Anniversary of the Incorporation of the Pennsylvania Railroad Company. Philadelphia: Pennsylvania Railroad, 1896.

All Stations: A Journey Through 150 Years of Railway History. Paris: Science Museum (London), 1978.

Encyclopedia of American Business History and Biography: Railroads in the Nineteenth Century. New York: Bruccoli Clark Layman, Inc., and Facts on File, Inc., 1988.

The Central Mass. Reading, MA: The Boston & Maine Railroad Historical Society, Inc., 1975.

Alexander, Edwin P. *The Pennsylvania Railroad: A Pictorial History*, 1st ed. New York: W. W. Norton, 1947.

——. *Down at the Depot: American Railroad Stations from 1831 to 1920.* New York: Bramhall House, 1952.

Baedeker, Karl. *Baedeker's The United States: Handbook for Travelers.* Leipzig: Karl Baedeker Publishing, 1909.

Beck, John. *Never Before in History: The Story of Scranton.* Northridge, CA: Windsor Publications, 1986.

Behrend, George. *Railway Holiday in France.* Newton Abbot: David and Charles, 1964.

Biddle, Gordon. *Great Railway Stations of Britain.* Newton Abbot: David and Charles, 1986.

Binney, Marcus, and David Pearce, eds. *Railway Architecture.* London: Bloomsbury Books, 1979.

Boag, George, L. *The Railways of Spain.* London: The Railway Gazette, 1923.

Bradley, Bill. *The Last of the Great Stations: 40 Years of the Los Angeles Union Passenger Terminal.* Burbank, CA: Interurban Press, 1979.

Burgess, George, H., and Miles C. Kennedy. *Centennial History of the Pennsylvania Railroad.* Philadelphia: Pennsylvania Railroad, 1949.

Carroll, Brian. *Australia's Railway Days.* Melbourne: The Macmillan Company of Australia PTY LTD, 1976.

Carter, Ernest F. *Famous Railway Stations of the World—and Their Traffic.* London: Frederick Muller, Ltd., 1958.

Casey, Robert J., and W.A.S. Douglas. *The Lackawanna Story.* New York: McGraw-Hill, 1951.

Churella, Albert. *The Pennsylvania Railroad, Vol. 1: Building an Empire, 1846–1917.* City University of Pennsylvania Press, 2013.

Clarke, Thomas Curtis, et al. *The American Railway: Its Construction, Development, Management, and Appliances.* New York: Scribner's, 1889.

Condit, Carl. *Port of New York, Vols. 1 & 2.* Chicago: University of Chicago Press, 1980, 1981.

Diehl, Lorraine B. *The Late Great Pennsylvania Station.* New York: Four Walls Eight Windows, 1985.

Doherty, Timothy Scott, and Brian Solomon. *Conrail.* St Paul: MBI Publishing, 2004.

Dorsey, Edward Bates. *English and American Railroads Compared.* New York: John Wiley & Sons, 1887.

Droege, John A. *Freight Terminals and Trains.* New York: McGraw-Hill Book Company, 1912.

——. *Passenger Terminals and Trains.* New York: McGraw-Hill Book Company, 1916.

Drury, George H. *The Historical Guide to North American Railroads.* Waukesha, WI: Kalmbach Books, 1985.

Dubin, Arthur D. *More Classic Trains.* Milwaukee: Kalmbach Publishing Co., 1974.

——. *Some Classic Trains.* Milwaukee: Kalmbach Publishing Co., 1964.

Duke, Donald. *Union Pacific in Southern California 1890–1990.* San Marino, CA: Golden West Books, 2005.

Duke, Donald, and Stan Kistler. *Santa Fe: Steel Rails Through California.* San Marino, CA: Golden West Books, 1963.

Dunscomb, Guy, L. *A Century of Southern Pacific Steam Locomotives.* Modesto, CA: privately printed, 1963.

Fischler, Stan. *Next Stop Grand Central.* Ontario: Boston Mills Press, 1986.

Frailey, Fred W. *Twilight of the Great Trains.* Waukesha, WI: Kalmbach Publishing Co., 1998.

Gruber, John, and Brian Solomon. *The Milwaukee Road's Hiawathas.* St. Paul: MBI Publishing, 2006.

Hare, Jay V. *History of the Reading.* Philadelphia: John Henry Strock, 1966.

Harlow, Alvin F. *Steelways of New England.* New York: Creative Age Press, 1946.

Hirota, Naotaka. *The Lure of Japan's Railways.* Tokyo: Japan Times, 1969.

Hofsommer, Don. L. *The Road of the Century.* New York: Creative Age Press, 1947.

——. *Southern Pacific 1900–1985.* College Station, TX: A&M University Press, 1986.

Hollander, Stanley, C. *Passenger Transportation.* Lansing, Michigan: Michigan State University, 1968.

Holton, James L. *The Reading Railroad: History of a Coal Age Empire, Vols. I & II.* Laurys Station, PA: Garrigues House, 1992.

Hungerford, Edward. *Men of Erie.* New York: Random House, 1946.

Jackson, Alan, A. *London's Termini.* Newton Abbot: David & Charles (Publishers) Limited, 1969.

Jones, Robert C. *The Central Vermont Railway, Vols. I–VII.* Shelburne, VT: New England Press, 1995.

Jones, Robert W. *Boston & Albany: The New York Central in New England, Vols. 1 & 2.* Los Angeles: Pine Tree Press, 1997.

Lamb, W. Kaye. *History of the Canadian Pacific Railway.* New York: Macmillan, 1977.

McPherson, Logan Grant. *Transportation in Europe.* New York: Holt and Company, 1910.

Meeks, Carroll L.V. *The Railroad Station.* New Haven, CT: Yale University Press, 1956.

Middleton, William D. *Grand Central . . . the World's Greatest Railway Terminal.* San Marino, CA: Golden West Books, 1977.

——. *Landmarks on the Iron Road.* Bloomington: Indiana University Press, 1999.

——. *Manhattan Gateway: New York's Pennsylvania Station.* Waukesha, WI: Kalmbach Books, 1996.

——. *Metropolitan Railways: Rapid Transit in America.* Bloomington and Indianapolis: Indiana University Press, 2003.

——. *When the Steam Railroads Electrified.* Milwaukee: Kalmbach, 1974.

Middleton, William D., with George M. Smerk, and Roberta L. Diehl. *Encyclopedia of North American Railroads.* Bloomington and Indianapolis: Indiana University Press, 2007.

Mott, Edward Harold. *Between the Ocean and the Lakes: The Story of Erie.* New York: John S. Collins, 1900.

Oshsner, Jeffery Karl. *H.H. Richardson Complete Architectural Works.* Cambridge: MIT Press, 1982.

Pearson, J. P. *Railways and Scenery, Series 1, Vols. I–IV.* London: Cassell and Company, Ltd., 1932.

Pietrak, Paul V., with Joseph G. Streamer and James A. Van Brocklin. *Western New York and Pennsylvania Railway.* Hamburg, NY: privately published, 2000.

Potter, Janet Greenstein. *Great American Railroad Stations.* New York: John Wiley & Sons, 1996.

Protheroe, Ernest. *The Railways of the World.* London: George Routledge & Sons, Ltd., 1920.

Rosenberger, Homer Tope. *The Philadelphia and Erie Railroad.* Potomac, MD: The Fox Hills Press, 1975.

Roth, Leland M. *Understanding Architecture: Its Elements, History, and Meaning.* Boulder, CO: Westview Press, 1993.

Rowe, D. Trevor. *Railway Holiday in Portugal.* Newton Abbot: David and Charles, 1966.

——. *Spain & Portugal.* London: Ian Allen, 1970.

Rowe, Vivian. *French Railways of To-Day.* London: George G. Harrap & Co. Ltd., 1958.

Ryan, Dennis, and Joseph Shine. *Southern Pacific Passenger Trains, Vols. 1 & 2.* La Mirada, CA: Four Ways West Publications, 2000.

Saylor, Roger B. *The Railroads of Pennsylvania.* State College: Pennsylvania State University, 1964.

Saunders, Richard, Jr. *Main Lines: American Railroads 1970–2002.* DeKalb, Illinois: Northern Illinois University Press, 2003.

——. *Merging Lines: American Railroads 1900–1970.* DeKalb: Northern Illinois University Press, 2001.

——. *The Railroad Mergers and the Coming of Conrail.* Westport, CT: Greenwood-Heineman Publishing, 1978.

Schafer, Mike, and Brian Solomon. *Pennsylvania Railroad.* Minneapolis: Voyageur Press, 2009.

Shaughnessy, Jim. *Delaware & Hudson.* Berkeley, CA: Howell North Books, 1967.

——. *The Rutland Road,* 2nd ed. Syracuse, NY: Syracuse University Press, 1997.

Simburger, Edward J. *A Complete Guide to the Los Angeles Metrolink Commuter Train System.* Agoura, CA: Yerba Seca, 1996.

Snell, J. B. *Early Railways.* London, 1972.

Solomon, Brian. *The American Diesel Locomotive.* Osceola, Wisconsin: MBI Publishing, 2000.

——. *The American Steam Locomotive.* Osceola, WI: MBI Publishing, 1998.

——. *Amtrak.* St. Paul: MBI Publishing, 2004.

——. *Burlington Northern Santa Fe Railway.* St. Paul: MBI Publishing, 2005.

——. *CSX.* St. Paul: MBI Publishing, 2005.

——. *Locomotive.* Osceola, WI: MBI Publishing, 2001.

——. *North American Railroads: The Illustrated Encyclopedia.* Minneapolis: Voyageur Press, 2012.

——. *Railroad Signaling.* St. Paul: MBI Publishing, 2003.

——. *Railroad Stations.* New York: MetroBooks, 1998.

——. *Railway Masterpieces: Celebrating the World's Greatest Trains, Stations, and Feats of Engineering.* Iola, WI: Krause Publishing, 2002.

Solomon, Brian, and Mike Schafer. *New York Central Railroad.* Osceola, WI: MBI Publishing, 1999.

Stilgoe, John R. *Metropolitan Corridor.* New Haven, CT: Yale University Press, 1983.

Stindt, Fred A. *The Northwestern Pacific Railroad: Redwood Empire Route.* Redwood City, CA: privately published, 1964.

——. *San Francisco's Century of Street Cars.* Kelseyville, CA: Stindt Books, 1990.

Taber, Thomas Townsend, III. *The Delaware, Lackawanna & Western Railroad, Parts I & II.* Williamsport, PA: privately published, 1980.

Talbot, F. A. *Railway Wonders of the World, Volumes 1 & 2.* London: Cassell & Co., 1914.

Thompson, Gregory Lee. *The Passenger Train in the Motor Age.* Columbus: Ohio State University Press, 1993.

Turner, Gregg M., and Melancthon W. Jacobus. *Connecticut Railroads.* Hartford: The Connecticut Historical Society, 1989.

Walker, Mike. *Steam Powered Video's Comprehensive Railroad Atlas of North America: Great Lakes West. U.S.A.* Feaversham, Kent, UK: Steam Powered Publishing, 1996.

Weller, John, L. *The New Haven Railroad: Its Rise and Fall.* New York: Hastings House, 1969.

Westing, Frederic. *Penn Station: Its Tunnels and Side Rodders.* Seattle: Superior Publishing, 1977.

Winchester, Clarence. *Railway Wonders of the World, Volumes 1 & 2.* London: The Waverley Book Company, Ltd., 1935.

Wright, Richard K. *Southern Pacific Daylight.* Thousand Oaks, CA: Wright Enterprises, 1970.

Young, William S. *Starrucca, the Bridge of Stone.* Privately published, 2000.

PERIODICALS

American Railroad Journal and Mechanics' Magazine (published in the 1830s and 1840s).

CTC Board, Ferndale, WA.

Jane's World Railway, London.

Moody's Analyses of Investments, Part I: Steam Railroads, New York.

Official Guide to the Railways, 1868–1969, New York.

Pacific RailNews, Waukesha, WI (no longer published).

Railroad History, formerly *Railway and Locomotive Historical Society Bulletin,* Boston.

Railway Age, Chicago and New York.

Gazette, 1870–1908, New York (no longer published).

The Railway Gazette, London.

Thomas Cook, European Timetable, Peterborough, UK (no longer published).

Today's Railways, Sheffield, UK.

TRAINS Magazine, Waukesha, WI.

Vintage Rails, Waukesha, WI (no longer published).

BROCHURES, MANUALS, TIMETABLES, RULE BOOKS, AND REPORTS

American Association of State Highway and Transportation Officials. *Freight-Rail Bottom Line Report.* 2003

Amtrak public time tables, 1971–2014.

Arnold, Bion Joseph. *Report on the Rearrangement and Development of the Steam Railroad Terminals in the City of Chicago.* Chicago, 1913.

Boston & Albany Railroad. *Time-Table No. 174.* 1955.

Boston & Albany Railroad. *Facts about the Boston & Albany R.R.* 1933

Chicago, Milwaukee, St. Paul & Pacific public time tables, 1943–1966.

Chicago Operating Rules Association. *Operating Guide.* [1994]

Conrail. *Pittsburgh Division, System Timetable No. 5.* 1997.

CSX Transportation. *Baltimore Division, Timetable No. 2.* 1987.

CSX Transportation System Map, 1999.

Delaware, Lackawanna & Western. *A Manual of the Delaware, Lackawanna & Western.* 1928.

Erie Railroad. *Erie Railroad: Its Beginnings and Today.* 1951.

Interstate Commerce Commission. *Fourth Annual Report on the Statistics of Railways of the United States for the Year Ended June 30, 1891.* Washington, DC, 1892

New York Central System public time tables, 1943–1968.

Northeast Operating Rules Advisory Committee. *NORAC Operating Rules,* 7th ed. 2000

Pennsylvania Railroad public time tables, 1942–1968.

Santa Fe public time tables, 1943–1969.

Southern Pacific Company. *Pacific System Time Table No. 17, Coast Division.* 1896.

Southern Pacific Company public time tables, 1930–1958.

Southern Pacific. *Your Daylight Trip.* 1939.

Steamtown National Historic Site. *The Nation's Living Railroad Museum.* n.d.

INDEX

ABOUT BRIAN SOLOMON

Brian Solomon earned a Bachelor of Fine Arts degree in Narrative Documentary Photographic Illustration from the Rochester Institute of Technology. In addition to a career in professional photography, he served as editor of *Pacific RailNews* and as associate editor of *Passenger Train Journal*. Since the mid-1990s, he has worked as a freelance author and completed more than fifty book projects and dozens of magazine articles, while traveling extensively in North America and Europe. Since 1998, he has spent a portion of each year in Ireland, where he has photographed landscapes, architecture, and railways. Follow his daily railway-photo blog at www.briansolomon.com/trackingthelight.